FABLES & FAIRY TALES

Bullies vs the Bold

Educator Edition

Stories by **Chip Colquhoun**

Lessons by **Helen Simpson** & **Rob Small**

Illustrated by **Korky Paul** & **Mario Coelho**

EPIC TALES®
an immersive experience

Dedications

For William (because it can't be a bison)
– *Chip*

For Andy
– *Helen*

For Sarah, my amazing wife
– *Rob*

For Craigie, with love
– *Korky*

For the amazing mother of my daughters
– *Mario*

Contents

Story-Led Learning Fundamentals

First time using a *Fables & Fairy Tales* Educator Edition? Start here.

If you're reading this, chances are you already know, suspect, or have heard that stories are the most effective, efficient, and engaging of teaching tools. Researchers are repeatedly proving this to be true. For instance, in a 2013 controlled study by European Lifelong Learning, the average test result was 26% higher for a group of learners aged 10 and 11 when taught using a story-led approach, compared to standard rote methods.

This book, and indeed this series, is entirely practical, focused solely on enabling you to capitalise on the effectiveness of story-led learning for the benefit of your learners. As such, we won't be exploring the evidence justifying this approach here. If you'd like to expand your knowledge in this area (which we highly recommend, for knowledge is power!), please read the *All the Better to* books – especially the first in that series, *All the Better to Read You With*.

However, if you're starting *here* with the story-led approach, we're confident you'll quickly see the evidence yourself. Your learners will soon be remembering more, solving problems faster, and even enjoying their time in school.

In brief, here's how it works: You pick an Age Range, Subject, and Learning Objective that aligns with your curriculum, then share the associated story with your learners either in full or in part (the Lesson Plan will advise you). You read the tale using traditional storytelling techniques that have enthralled audiences for millennia (don't panic – we share those with you in the section on 'How to Use Your VOICE'), and then channel that engagement into relevant and purposeful learning activities.

For the greatest chance of success, there are just three fundamentals you need to keep in mind...

Fundamental 1: **Put the Story First**

We've heard far too many educators complain, "We just don't have time in the day to use stories." This issue arises because stories are seen as a kind of treat for the end of the day, after the 'hard work' is done – so when the work proves *too* hard, the treat gets dismissed or forgotten.

But the reason why stories are a treat is exactly why they should come *right at the start* of your learning. Stories ignite the curiosity and enthusiasm of young learners – the very qualities you want them to be demonstrating when they explore that set text, conduct that science experiment, tackle the next level of mathematics, etc.

So why waste that energy? Put the story at the start of your teaching session, and you'll soon have your learners in precisely the right mindset for learning more about topics covered in the story – whether they involve numeracy, literacy, or any other kind of knowledge.

Note: Very occasionally, a lesson will require you to lead an activity before beginning the story. For these situations, you should still aspire to create an atmosphere suited for storytelling – for which the next two fundamentals will help you prepare...

Fundamental 2:
Create a Storytelling Space

The best space for reading these stories is one without tables and chairs. Some older learners feel genuinely uncomfortable sitting on a carpet; if so, allowing them lie on their sides is better than letting them slouch on chairs.

If moving tables and chairs out of the way is impossible, try to find another space where sitting on the floor is both possible and comfortable. If you really must use a space where tables will be in the way, that's fine – but be aware that you'll need to put extra energy into ensuring the lesson feels *nothing like* a lesson, so your learners can be more open to relaxing and enjoying the activity.

Best of all, involve your learners in creating your storytelling space. Even just laying some paper around them, together with pencils for them to illustrate the story *if they want to* (be sure to stress that last part so it doesn't sound like an obligation) will help them feel more invested in the telling. And as we know from property, business, and romance, the more we invest in something, the more we care about it.

When sharing the stories, sit all your learners to face you *and only you*. While 'story circles' are a common idea, they're actually conducive to *distraction* rather than engagement – it's too easy for your learners to focus on each other rather than you and the story. Moreover, you'll find it harder to give your attention to all your learners at once, since some will always be slightly outside your natural field of vision – and that will make it harder for you to use Fundamental 3...

Fundamental 3:
Read *With* Your Learners, Not *To* Them

We call this 'the Keyring Skill', because it is the *only* principle you need to keep in mind to read like an engaging storyteller – whether using the stories from this book or elsewhere.

A performer knows they've done a good job when all eyes and/or ears have been focused on them, and when (if it's a live performance) they receive rapturous applause at the end.

A *storyteller* knows they've done a good job when they detect signs that their listeners have engaged with the experience – such as immediate questions about decisions taken by the characters, the truth of the events, the story's origins, etc. All this shows that the listeners were focused more on the story than the performance.

Of course, everyone's signs of engagement are different. For some, it's an ardent stare. For others, it's closed eyes and a faint smile. For yet others, it's sharing an expression, or even words, with someone nearby.

Using your Keyring Skill effectively means being aware of your audience, far more than requiring *them* to be aware of *you*.

Your prior knowledge of your learners will help hugely with this. For instance, if you're reading an animal story to a group that includes learners who love physical activity, why not ask those learners to demonstrate what it might be like to move as those animals? If you're reading a fantasy story to a group including science enthusiasts, why not pause to discuss what real-life solutions could let us recreate magic like levitation, conjuring, etc? And if your group includes someone who loves drawing, why not give that learner a pencil and paper and ask them to illustrate the story as you read it?

In short, allowing each learner to engage in their own way will vastly increase the level of their engagement, regardless of the tale.

The next section shares some techniques to help you 'read like a storyteller' and attain a high level of engagement with any story. But if you're in a rush to skip to the stories and lessons, use these fundamentals and you can't go wrong.

How to Use Your VOICE

Five traditional storytelling techniques to easily engage your learners

Please don't be put off by the title of this section – we don't mean 'put on an accent' or anything like that. Changing your entire voice to sound like a character is a performance technique. It may result in greater engagement with you, but it can actually result in worse engagement with *the story* – because your learners will be more focused on your prowess as a performer than on the tale you're trying to tell.

Instead, we offer VOICE as an acronym for five key storytelling skills to hang from your *Keyring* Skill (see the previous two pages, if you haven't already). These are...

Vocal Adjustments
Openings
Indication
Conversation
Environment

Before we explore these in more detail, please keep this in mind throughout: **none of these are essential.** Being 'key' means they *can* unlock engagement – but sometimes the keys won't fit. Your learners may not care for any of these techniques – or, as is more often the case, *the story alone will be engaging enough.* Use your Keyring Skill to decide.

That said, let's share some of the best insights that the world of traditional storytelling can offer to those who plan to read aloud for an audience...

Vocal Adjustments

This is something you do all the time, usually without thinking about it. If you're concerned, you lower your pitch; if you're excited, you increase your pace; if you're trying to get someone's attention across a crowded room, you project.

For those on the receiving end, there's an almost universal unconscious understanding of what these Vocal Adjustments mean. Someone speaks to you with a lower pitch than usual? You probably want to know what's wrong. Someone's speaking too fast? You may need to ask them to slow down so you can understand why they're so excited. A loud voice cuts across a great distance? You turn to look, checking whether it's your attention they want.

So if all this nuance of language can be transmitted automatically, you can be sure of enhancing your reading by putting just a little thought into it in advance. When reading a passage, consider how it's making *you* feel. How would you adjust your voice if trying to convey that same feeling? Try reading the passage out loud with that same Vocal Adjustment, and you'll share the same emotion with your listeners.

You can apply this approach to characters in a story, too. What emotion is the *character* feeling? How would you adjust *your* voice to convey such a feeling? Read their dialogue with that same Vocal Adjustment, and all your listeners will feel a greater understanding for the character.

Openings

If you're confident that your listeners will predict the next word, then preceding it with the inflexion of a question mark, along with a slight pause, can prompt them to say it for (or with) you.

Doing this gives you an opportunity to confirm the engagement of your listeners – but not just for you. When they hear *themselves* providing the right response, they'll be recognising their *own* engagement. Essentially, this will give rise to a 'feedback loop': hearing themselves (and others) engaging with the tale will encourage them to engage even more.

In the stories in this series, we often include a clue in the punctuation to let you know the best moments to use an Opening. If you haven't quite reached the end of a sentence or a paragraph, but you find yourself coming across an ellipsis (...) followed by a question mark, that's an...?

Opening – exactly.

In all instances where we suggest Openings, give it a try. We're confident that your learners will respond if they're able to do so.

Indication

Let's say you're listening to someone telling a story about a spider. They say, "This story is about a very small creature..." – and, at the same time, hold out a closed hand that *isn't quite* a fist. They look at their hand, and add, "...who was actually..."

Slowly, they open their fingers, palm towards the ceiling.

"...a *spider*," they finish.

In that moment, what are you imagining to be in their hand?

Even without the presence of an actual arachnid, the storyteller's gesture has guided your imagination to create an *Indication* of one. And if your listeners are creating, they're *investing in the experience of your story* – which is the very definition of engagement.

Indication works best when it combines three core elements...

1. **a physical gesture** (e.g. a hand held out);

2. **a *suggestion of mass*** (e.g. by not fully closing the hand); and

3. **the teller's *sight line*** (e.g. looking at their hand).

Of these, item 3 is the most important. If you look up as if you're seeing an elephant and declare, "The elephant stood up!" then your audience will be more convinced that you are Indicating an elephant standing up. That, in turn, will encourage *them* to envision the same – even though you haven't used a physical gesture, nor given any suggestion of mass.

Conversation

As you go through the story, invite your listeners to comment on it, say what *they* think is about to happen, what *they* would do in a similar situation, etc. There is quite simply no better method of confirming and compounding the engagement of your audience.

Conversation needn't just be about the story, either. It can also cover the *telling* of the story. For instance, when deciding on a Vocal Adjustment for a character, you can ask your listeners to suggest how that character might sound. You can ask them how they think the *Environment* should sound. You could even simply ask them if there's anything they'd like to do to feel more involved in the story, such as turning up the lights so they can see you more easily – or turning them *down* for a *spooky* story...

There are two important factors to consider when using this key skill. The first is to avoid giving your audience any suggestion of *control* over the story. For example, instead of asking, "What happens next?", your question should be, "What *do you think* will happen next?" By doing so, you'll avoid the potential of engagement-busting disappointment when you read on to reveal an action that entirely contradicts your listener's suggestion. You'll also avoid any sense of competition between the ideas of your listeners. If all you invited was their *thoughts*, you can legitimately move on with the words, "Shall we find out?"

The second factor is knowing when to move on. Don't lose sight of the fact that you're telling a story – and you need time to finish it!

Conversation may be the most powerful key skill on your keyring. To help you use it, you'll often find questions *written into* the stories within this series. When you come to these questions, take time to gather some responses from your learners.

Environment

The final key skill we'll share with you here is the easiest form of audience participation: inviting your listeners to create the story *Environment* with you.

We don't just mean the look and/or feel of the location where you're sharing your stories, which was covered in Fundamental 2 of the previous section. A big part of the Environment is in fact *your learners themselves* – so why not use them?

For example, you read that a wind is blowing through the trees. Why not invite your learners to make the sound of that breeze? By contributing to the atmosphere of the story, they'll feel further invested in it. Don't worry about silencing them afterwards, either – just continue to read, raising your voice ever so slightly *if needed*, and you'll soon find your learners quietening down naturally in order to discover the action that takes place in the setting they've helped to establish.

Letting learners join in with repeated phrases can also add to the story Environment. When they join in with a refrain, they get that 'feedback loop' on their engagement again: they hear that they've learned a piece of the story, confirming that they paid some attention – and so they pay even more.

One of the reasons refrains are a great form of Environment participation is because you will likely find you don't have to invite your learners to join in. Indeed, issuing an invitation can sometimes *break* engagement, because you're taking your learners out of the world of the story and back into the classroom, asking them to consider an instruction from their educator.

When you first encounter the refrain, boldly perform your action. The second time, add a slight Opening to the start of it. Do this again for your third time, and many of your learners will begin to join in. From that point on, you'll probably find most if not all are eagerly participating.

In this series, you'll occasionally come across phrases printed in **<u>bold and underlined text</u>**. These are our suggestions for when your learners could join in with you – be it by saying the words along with you, joining in with a repeated action, or both. Before reading the story to your learners, take some time to plan and consider an action that will be appropriate, easy, and comfortable to repeat, so you're ready when it comes up in the reading.

Never Forget Your Keyring

We're fairly confident that all the key storytelling techniques described here will be easy for you to deploy in your own reading – and we hope you are too.

But always keep in mind that each of these skills is *optional*. Some won't fit in every story, and some won't fit with every *audience*. As always, the *keyring* rule is**...?**

Read *with* your learners, not *to* them. Select your key skills based on your knowledge of what is likely to work with *your* learners.

Always hold onto that thought, and it won't be long before, first, you hear your learners describe you as "the best storyteller ever...!"

...and, second, you believe them.

Planning Your Lessons

The Age Ranges in this book are a guide only. You are welcome to adapt any lesson for the specific needs of your unique cohort of learners.

As you flick through the lesson plans, you'll notice that each one has a flag in the upper left-hand corner to show where the story fits in relation to the lesson content. They are...

Lesson First

In rare cases, the lesson will need to be completed entirely before the story begins. The story could be seen as a reward for your learners attempting that lesson's activities.

This need not prevent you using the lesson if you have shared the story previously. You may find your learners are excited by the prospect of hearing it again, but you could also try retelling it with even more of their involvement – e.g. dramatising it as you go by casting your learners as the characters.

However, to help you with your planning, any lessons like this will be at the start of each Age Group for that story's lesson plans.

Story Pause

Sometimes, the plan will recommend beginning the lesson with the story, and then pausing at a marker specified by the lesson plan. These markers will always be easy to identify, being singled-out, emboldened, and centred in the text with a different font to the story text – e.g.

<4+ M1>

At that point, you will set an activity (or activities) for your learners to do. Continuing the story could then be seen as a reward for completing that activity.

Again, this need not prevent you using the lesson if you have shared the story previously. In fact, if you let your learners know that you're only going to retell a little of the story, and add that "You'll soon see why...", this may be an extra hook with which to engage them.

However, because the story may have multiple pause markers, these lesson plans will appear in the order of those markers. That way you could stretch out the story across several days to cover a variety of topics.

Notice, though, that we said "the plan will **recommend**" this option. That's because, with a little tweaking, you can use these plans much like the next set, which are...

Story First

If you see this last flag, it means the story will need to be shared with your learners in full, before the Starter/Prior Knowledge Check ***and/or*** the Main Input of the lesson begins – so be prepared to factor in the reading time when working out how long the lesson is likely to take for your learners.

That's it for the preamble! You may now want to flick straight to the lessons to decide which ones you'll do when – but as soon as you have time, we recommend you take a moment to sample the stories...

The REAL King of the Jungle

Based on an Indian folk tale
Adapted & written by Chip Colquhoun
Illustrated by Korky Paul

Some people once got very scared in the Indian jungle. The thick and twisty plants covering the bumpy ground were making their journey hard, and there weren't enough trees to hide from the blazing sun – so they felt more and more tired and dizzy.

That's why, when a lion burst out from a bush and surprised them, they panicked, and ran as fast as they could until they found a village.

Those people told everyone that the lion was huge and monstrous, and soon everyone said that the lion must be "the King of the Jungle".

But the animals in the jungle knew better. *They* knew that Jungle Lion was just an overgrown kitty-cat. Even Jungle Lion would say he'd only wanted to ask the people if they had a hairbrush for his knotted mane. Then he'd say, "Oh, you want the King Lion? You need to go to the African Savannah. There are no King Lions here."

You see, all the animals in the Indian jungle knew *exactly* who their king was – and any of them could tell you the story of how he became king in the first place...

<4+ G1>

At the start of this story, Tenduay the Leopard was smaller than Jungle Lion – but he had ten times the appetite. Being smaller also meant he could be swifter and sneakier through the thick and twisty plants blanketing the bumpy ground – and this made him better at catching animals for his food.

Much better. Tenduay had an antelope for breakfast, a monkey for a mid-morning snack, *two* antelopes for lunch, and a little red panda for afternoon tea. For each one there'd be a chase – ***swoosh!*** – a claw – ***swipe!*** – and lastly, Tenduay's jaws – ***chomp chomp chomp.***

For dinner, Tenduay chose between an elephant, a rhinoceros, or a the type of Indian cow known as a gaur. Sometimes he ate all three. ***Swoosh! Swipe! Chomp chomp chomp.***

For pudding, he decided between a python, a crocodile, or a duck. Sometimes he devoured all three. ***Swoosh! Swipe! Chomp chomp chomp.***

Finally, for supper, he selected from a hare, a pangolin, or a loris. Sometimes he gorged upon all three. ***Swoosh! Swipe! Chomp chomp chomp.***

<4+ S1>

<4+ M1>

Tenduay's greed soon made the jungle look very untidy indeed. There weren't as many antelopes, hares, or gaurs to eat the plants covering the ground, so they grew from thick and twisty to something even worse: dense and tangled. And since there were fewer elephants, rhinos, or lorises to eat the leaves, the trees got so heavy that they bent towards the ground. Some even snapped and fell over.

With a shortage of red pandas and pangolins to munch on the bugs, there were so many creepy-crawlies wriggling and skittering around that everyone was itching terribly. And with a dearth of monkeys and ducks to spread seeds, there weren't enough new trees and plants to replace the dying ones. Lots of dead plants meant even more skittering bugs – like beetles, worms, and woodlice.

But that wasn't all. After eating most of his food, Tenduay left his leftovers hanging from the branches of trees – so he could come back later for seconds. This meant raw meat dangled all around the jungle – and *that* meant loads of flies buzzing around too.

Something had to be done. One day, all the jungle animals met up to discuss the matter – all except Tenduay. They met immediately after a heavy rain shower, because they knew Tenduay wouldn't be around. Tenduay *really* didn't like getting wet.

Being the largest animal there, Elephant spoke first. “Friends of the jungle,” she said. “We all know Tenduay the Leopard is eating far too much, and the jungle we call home is suffering.”

Monkey interrupted. “But what can we do? None of us can fight Tenduay. Me and Hare are too small. You and Rhino are big, but too slow. Gaur and Antelope are just the right size, but they don’t have the right teeth for fighting.”

Red Panda was nervously watching Lion and the carnivorous reptiles. “What about Lion? *He* has the right teeth…”

Lion slowly shook his head. “We lions don’t have the energy. Tenduay has been eating so much, he’s taken most of the food from us – so we are all weak.”

“The same is true for us,” Crocodile added. “How do you think Tenduay has been able to sneak up and eat us for pudding?”

“But Gaur and Antelope have long horns,” Python said. “Surely *they* can fight Tenduay?”

Gaur shook her head sadly. “Tenduay is too fast for us. We just have to face it: Tenduay is going to destroy our entire habitat.”

“No,” Elephant stated firmly. “Tenduay has to understand that if the jungle dies, we *all* die – including him. We must make a deal with him. Here’s what I suggest…”

Elephant explained her idea. The other animals were shocked and scared at first, but soon they all agreed: there was no other way.

Elephant then trumpeted a loud call for Tenduay through her trunk.

Tenduay went along. He wasn’t scared of all the animals standing together. He knew he could kill them all if he had to. “What’s this all about?” he asked. “Hurry up. I’m getting hungry…”

Elephant spoke firmly. “Tenduay, your greed is killing the jungle. Look around: the grass is getting too long, the trees are getting too heavy, no new plants are growing, and everywhere is crawling with bugs and flies.”

Tenduay shrugged. “So? That’s not my problem. My only problem is what I’m having for lunch.”

But Elephant remained resolute. "Both those problems are the same, Tenduay. If the jungle dies, you won't *have* any lunch."

That made Tenduay pause. If he couldn't get lunch in the jungle, he would have to move home. And then he might have to fight some of the other big cats – like the strongest of all: Tiger...

Irritated, Tenduay growled. "What do you want me to do, then?"

Elephant gave one last look to the other animals. They all nodded, so she told him, "From now on, you won't need to chase us. We will come to you. At midday every day, one of us will meet you at the giant mahua tree by the watering hole – and you can eat that animal.

"We will draw bamboo shoots to choose a new animal for you each day. Because you won't have to hunt us, one animal should be enough – and that will allow the jungle to recover.

"Do you agree?"

Tenduay thought about this a moment, then looked at all the animals one by one. They were all trying to look brave, but Tenduay could see them all shaking – even Lion.

So Tenduay grinned. "Yes, I agree – on two conditions. First, you must send *three* animals each day—"

"But—" Elephant tried to interrupt.

Tenduay quickly held up a paw to shut her up. "*One* for me to eat, one to give me a song or a story, and another to give me a wash. If I can't hunt, I'll need some other way to have fun – and if you want me to save energy, I can't wash myself."

Elephant looked around at the other animals. They all shrugged nervously. She looked back at Tenduay and said, "Fine. And your other condition?"

Tenduay's grin vanished, and he growled, "*Do not* be late. If one of you arrives so much as a *minute* after midday, I'll eat *every single one of you!* And this jungle can disappear forever..."

The animals flinched, and stared in frightened silence – until, at last, Elephant nodded. Then Crocodile nodded, then Gaur – and soon, everyone had nodded.

"We will never be late," Elephant assured Tenduay. "We all want the jungle to survive."

With that, the animals all went their separate ways – and Tenduay went to the giant mahua tree by the watering hole.

The next morning, the animals gathered again. Elephant held up a bunch of bamboo shoots in her trunk. Each animal took one with their eyes shut, then held them out to see who had taken the shortest.

<7+ M1>

Gaur held the shortest bamboo. "Oh well," she said. "I guess I'm getting eaten today."

Antelope held the next shortest bamboo. "I hope Tenduay likes my song," she said.

Red Panda held the next shortest. "Uck! I have to wash that stinky creep? I hope I don't ruin the shine on my lovely red fur..."

So Gaur, Antelope, and Red Panda rushed to the watering hole to get there for midday.

<4+ M2>

Gaur and Antelope had strong, sturdy legs to travel steadily on the bumpy ground, so *they* wouldn't be late. And Red Panda was small and nimble to scurry through the dense and tangled plants. *He* wouldn't be late either.

Sure enough, they arrived in time for midday. Tenduay immediately set upon Gaur with a**...?** ***Swoosh! Swipe! Chomp chomp chomp.***

Then Tenduay lay back and listened to Antelope's song, while Red Panda scrubbed the sweat and mud from his fur.

The next morning, the animals gathered yet again. Elephant held up another clump of bamboo shoots in her trunk. Each animal took one at random, then compared them to see who had taken the shortest.

Elephant held the shortest bamboo. "Oh well," she said. "I guess it's my turn today."

Monkey held the next shortest. "I'm sure I can think of a story Tenduay will like," she said.

Duck held the next shortest. "Washing isn't so bad for me," he said. "I'm used to water!"

So Elephant, Monkey, and Duck rushed to the watering hole to get there for midday. Elephant had strong, sturdy legs that were twice the size of Antelope's – so *she* certainly wouldn't be late. Monkey swung through the trees to get there. *She* wouldn't be late either.

Duck just swam along the river. There was no chance of *him* being late.

Sure enough, they all arrived in time for midday. Tenduay immediately set upon Elephant with a...? ***Swoosh! Swipe! Chomp chomp chomp.***

Then Tenduay lay back and listened to Monkey's story, while Duck used his feathers to wipe the sweat and mud from Tenduay's fur.

The next morning, the animals gathered once more. Elephant (a different elephant, of course) held up another assortment of bamboo shoots in her trunk. Each animal took one at random, then contrasted them to see who had taken the shortest.

Loris held the shortest bamboo. "Aw," he said. "I didn't plan to be eaten today. But oh well, it's all for the good of the jungle."

Crocodile held the next shortest bamboo. "I'm no good at singing *or* storytelling," she said. "I hope Tenduay won't mind me drumming..."

Python held the next shortest. "How am I supposed to wash him without any arms?" she wondered out loud. "Oh well. I suppose I'll have to find a way."

So Loris, Crocodile, and Python started on their way to the watering hole to get there for midday. Both Crocodile and Python moved fastest in water, so they both set off along the river. *They* wouldn't be late.

Loris, though, wasn't used to travelling fast in the sun. He usually stayed close to the trees, so he could always hide in the shadows – but to reach the watering hole, he had to traverse some treeless plains.

The sunlight dazzled his big round eyes, making it hard to see where he was going. Whenever he stopped to look, he realised he'd gone round in a circle! And it was a long way for his little legs. Soon he was dizzy, weary, and worried.

<4+ M3>

Loris tried to move faster. At last, he spotted the giant mahua tree sticking up from the horizon. He rushed to it as fast as he could.

When Loris arrived at the watering hole, he found Tenduay there all alone.

"Oh," Loris said. "Where are Crocodile and Python?"

"They're here..." Tenduay replied calmly – then boomed, "*...in my* ***belly!***"

Tenduay began to circle Loris, sneering, "You are *very* late, Loris! You know what that means? It means I now have to eat everyone in the jungle, and it's all *your* fault. *You* will be responsible for the death of the whole jungle! And I'll start with you..."

Loris may have had slow legs, but his mind worked fast. "Wait!" Loris said quickly. "It's the leopard's fault, not mine!"

Tenduay paused. "The leopard's fault? You're saying it's *my* fault?! Why you–"

"Not *you*, Tenduay," Loris replied hastily. "The *other* leopard! The leopard I met on my way here!"

Tenduay frowned. "*Another* leopard? *What* other leopard? I'm the only leopard in this jungle."

"You were," Loris agreed, "but as I made my way over here, I met another one. He threatened to eat me, so I told him I was on my way to meet you. That made him laugh, and he said you must be a weak leopard if you won't even hunt for your food."

"*What?!*" The orange fur on Tenduay's face began to turn red.

Loris nodded. "That's what I said! I told him you could catch *all* the animals in our jungle if you wanted! But he didn't believe me, and told me to bring you to him so he could challenge you – to a test of brawn."

"A test of what?" Tenduay asked.

"Brawn," Loris repeated. "I've never heard that word before either, but I *think* it means he wants to fight you to work out who's best."

Tenduay roared with rage, then got behind Loris. "Very well then!" he said. "Take me to this other leopard! I'll show *him* who's king around here...!"

"Th-th-th-this way..."

Loris took Tenduay along the riverbank. His mind was still running ten times as fast as his legs. His lie had got him this far – but how would he get away from Tenduay?

Tenduay growled impatiently. "Can't you go any faster?"

"I'm trying to remember the way," Loris replied apologetically.

Suddenly, Loris saw a cave beside the river. He pointed. "There! He went in there...!"

With another snarl, Tenduay leapt over Loris and ran to the cave. "Come out, coward!" he called. "Show yourself, phoney!"

There was no reply.

Tenduay peered into the cave...

…and there, looking up at him from below, was the other leopard.

Tenduay *ROARED!* – a thunderous bellow!

At exactly the same time, the other leopard roared back. He was definitely ready for a fight!

Well, thought Tenduay. *If it's a fight he wants, a fight he'll get!*

Tenduay thought quickly. The other leopard was almost exactly the same size as he was – with exactly the same markings too, in fact – but Tenduay had an advantage: he was higher up. With the other leopard below him, Tenduay could jump and land on the other leopard with all his claws – and have help from all his weight!

So Tenduay yelled, "Here I come, fiend!"

Tenduay *pounced* – and the other leopard pounced at exactly the same time.

Yes: *exactly* the same time.

Because it was exactly the same leopard.

Tenduay had been looking down at his own reflection in the water of a cave pool.

With a huge *SPLASH!*, Tenduay suddenly found himself surrounded by his biggest fear: *water!* And he didn't know how to swim…!

Loris didn't stay to find out what happened next. Instead, he made his way back to the jungle to let all the other animals know how he'd tricked Tenduay.

Tenduay was never seen again – at least, not in *that* jungle. Perhaps he was too ashamed of his foolishness, and ran away.

But all of the other animals cheered for Loris and his quick wit. From that day on, Loris and his family never had to travel fast to get anywhere, because they never had to run from anyone. Even today, there aren't many animals who will dare attack a slow loris.

And all the animals agree that *Loris* is the *real* king of the jungle. He bested a predator five times his size!

'REAL KING' LESSON PLANS

Ages 4+ Geography

Indian Jungle vs British Woodland

Learning Objective(s)

- To understand geographical similarities and differences through studying the human and physical geography of a small area of the United Kingdom and that of a contrasting non-European country.

Resources

- Cut out copies of the Jungle Feature cards from pages 22–23. These are:

  mahua tree - coconut tree - vines - bumpy ground
  lohita grandis - red panda - slow loris - leopard

  If you wish, you can include some of the Feature cards from page 29 also.

- Cut out copies of the Woodland Feature cards from pages 24–25. These are:

  oak tree - beech tree - willow tree - woodland ground
  stag beetle - rabbit - red squirrel - fox

  You should print enough Feature cards (Jungle and Woodland Features combined) for every learner/pair/group in your class to have at least one of ANY TYPE each.

- A large sheet of paper (e.g. spare backing paper) and thick marker pen.
- Various craft materials, e.g. sugar paper, tissue paper, white paper, glue sticks, felt tips
- Globe or world map (optional).

Preparation

- Take one of each Feature card, and mix them up into a single 'Discussion' pile.
- Mix up your remaining Feature cards into a separate single 'Activity' pile.

Starter – *"Do Now!"*

Hooks into learning

1. Read/continue/re-read 'The REAL King of the Jungle' to the mark **<4+ G1>** (optional, but highly recommended).
2. Ask your learners:

   "How is the Indian jungle different to a British woodland?"

   Optional: Show them how to locate the two countries on a globe or world map.

Main Input

1. Using the thick marker, draw a line down the centre of your large sheet of paper. Label one side 'Indian Jungle' and the other side 'British Woodland'.
2. Taking one card from your 'Discussion' pile at a time, share with your learners the feature's name and discuss what it is.
3. Discuss with your learners which side of the large sheet it should go on, i.e. Indian jungle or British woodland, then stick it to the appropriate side.
4. Repeat for the remaining 'Discussion' cards.
   After the first 2 or 3, you may wish to let individual learners choose the card, lead the discussion, and/or stick the image to the appropriate side.

Independent/Group Activity

1. Let your learners know you're all going to create two 3D artworks – one showing the features of an Indian jungle, the other showing features of a British woodland.
2. Allow each learner/pair/group to choose a card from your 'Activity' pile, and create a 3D version of that feature using the craft materials.
3. Encourage the learners to stick their completed feature on the correct side of your large sheet.
4. Learners who complete their feature early may choose another card to recreate in 3D.

Plenary

1. When the artworks are completed, attach a label to each feature written by your learners (or in your writing, with the learners' contributions).
2. Reward your learners for their work in this lesson by continuing to read the story!

Check In

Talk To Your Partner:

"What have you learnt today?"

Encourage your learners to share their thoughts. **We highly recommend this is the moment you share the Learning Objective with them, if at all.**

Jungle Feature Cards

Jungle Feature Cards

Woodland Feature Cards

Woodland Feature Cards

Story Pause

Ages 4+ Science (with bonus Phys.Ed.)
Jungle Food Chains

Learning Objective(s)

- To identify and name a variety of common animals.
- To describe how animals obtain their food from plants and other animals, using the idea of a simple food chain.
- To identify and name different sources of food.

Resources

- Fitness hoops.
- Sports bibs in 1–3 colours.
- Cut out copies of the Jungle Feature cards from pages 23 and 29. These are:

  lohita grandis - red panda - slow loris - leopard - jungle grass - hare - elephant - gaur

  If you wish, you can include Feature cards from page 22 also. You should print enough Feature cards for every learner/pair/group in your class to have at least one of EVERY TYPE each.
- Paper and pens/pencils.
- Gluesticks and/or sticky tape.

Preparation

This lesson requires a large space, so you may need to book your school hall or playground, or else push back all tables and chairs in your classroom. However, the lesson should still start in a space suitable for story reading.

Starter – *"Do Now!"*

Hooks into learning

1. Read/continue/re-read 'The REAL King of the Jungle' to the mark **<4+ S1>** (optional, but highly recommended).
2. Ask your learners:

   "Why does Tenduay have to eat the animals? Is it fair?"

   Open up a discussion about this, with your learners sharing their ideas and opinions.

Main Input

1. Let your learners know they are going to play 'The Food Chain Game'. Move to your **large space**, then divide them into Leopards (10%), Hares (30%), and Jungle Grasses (60%), using different coloured sports bibs to differentiate between them. Ask them to spread themselves out around the space.
   NB: If you don't have enough different colours, use jumpers/shirts to distinguish a further 1–2 groups.
2. Explain to the Jungle Grasses that they should stay in their spot unless collected by a Hare.
3. Give each hare a fitness hoop and explain this is their 'burrow'. If they are in their burrow, they can't be 'caught' by a Leopard. But to play the game, they must leave their burrow, collect a Jungle Grass, and bring it back to their burrow.
4. The Leopards have to try to tag the Hares. If a Hare is tagged by a Leopard, they must go to sit with you and are 'out'.
5. The game ends when all the 'food' (i.e. Jungle Grasses *or* Hares) has been collected or tagged.
6. After playing the game once, repeat it a few more times with different proportions, e.g. more Leopards but fewer Hares, fewer Jungle Grasses but more Hares, etc.
7. After each game, ask your learners what they observe going on when the amounts in each group changes.
8. Return to your smaller space (optional) and demonstrate the creation of a food chain by sticking relevant Feature cards onto a larger piece of paper, and adding arrows to show the direction of energy. It is recommended to begin with the food chain demonstrated in the game, i.e.

   Jungle Grasses → Hare → Leopard

   You may wish to also demonstrate a chain involving the beetle, e.g.

   Jungle Grasses → Lohita Grandis → Slow Loris → Leopard

   As you do so, help your learners to consider what each animal will eat.

Independent/Group Activity

Encourage your learners to create their own examples of food chains in the same way.

There's more...

Plenary

1. Model how to talk about your own work, explaining how you have arranged the elements of the food chain and why the arrows are in the direction they are.
2. Put each learner/group with another, and encourage them to share their thought process and what their work shows.
3. For Ages 7+: Invite your learners to write down how they might explain the food chain process to a younger learner.
4. Reward your learners for their work in this lesson by continuing to read the story!

Check In

Talk To Your Partner:

"What have you learnt today?"

Encourage your learners to share their thoughts. **We highly recommend this is the moment you share the Learning Objective with them, if at all.**

Additional Jungle Feature Cards

Story Pause

Ages 4+ Maths

Data Collection

Learning Objective(s)

- To interpret and construct simple tally charts/block diagrams.
- To ask and answer questions by counting the number of objects in each category.
- To ask and answer questions about totalling, and compare categorical data.

Resources

- Copies of the "Who Is Left?" worksheet from pages 32–33, enough for 1 per learner/pair/group. Note that this worksheet should be double-sided.
- A variety of Jungle Feature cards from pages 23 and 29 showing the following animals:

  hare - elephant - red panda - slow loris - gaur

  You should have different quantities of each animal.
- The example block graph from page 34.

Preparation

Place your animal Jungle Feature cards on display around the classroom in various locations.

Starter – *"Do Now!"*

Hooks into learning

1. Read/continue/re-read 'The REAL King of the Jungle' to the mark **<4+ M1>** (optional, but highly recommended).
2. Tell your learners that the Jungle Authorities are a bit worried about the jungle population following Tenduay's hungry rampage. They need your learners' help to collect data on the number of animals that are left.
3. Indicate the different animal images displayed around the room and discuss with your learners how they could collect this information.
4. If no one suggests it, model how to make a tally chart, counting some of the animals within easy view.
5. As individuals, in pairs, or in small groups, let your learners circulate around the room with their "Who is Left?" worksheets, collecting data on the number of animals left in the jungle using their tally charts.

Main Input

1. Call your learners back together to "share what we found out."
2. Explain that we need to organise this information carefully for the Jungle Authorities by making a block graph. Show them the example block graph and discuss what your learners notice.
3. Teach them about each different axis and explain what they mean. Check their understanding by asking a few questions about it..

Independent/Group Activity

Your learners use their tally charts to complete the Jungle Animal block graph, showing how many of each species of animal are left in the jungle. Then they answer the questions set at the bottom of the sheet.

Plenary

1. Share answers to the questions and explore how your learners found out. Model (and encourage them to use) full sentences to explain their ideas and reasoning.
2. Reward your learners for their work in this lesson by continuing to read the story!

Check In

Talk To Your Partner:

"What have you learnt today?"

Encourage your learners to share their thoughts. **We highly recommend this is the moment you share the Learning Objective with them, if at all.**

Who Is Left?

Side 1 of 2

How many animals are left in the jungle?

1. Record the number of each animal using a tally chart, like this: 卌

Animal	Tally
Elephant	
Slow Loris	
Hare	
Gaur	
Red Panda	

2. Then create a block graph to display the data.

10					
9					
8					
7					
6					
5					
4					
3					
2					
1					
	Elephant	Slow Loris	Hare	Gaur	Red Panda

Who Is Left?

Now answer these questions for the Jungle Authorities...

1. Which animal has the highest number left?

____

2. Which animal has the lowest number left?

____

3. How many animals are left altogether?

____

4. How many more elephants need to be born, to take the number back up to 10?

____

5. Are there more elephants or more hares left?

____

6. What is the difference between the number of gaurs and the number of hares left?

____

Example Block Graph

A graph to show the number of birds spotted during one day.

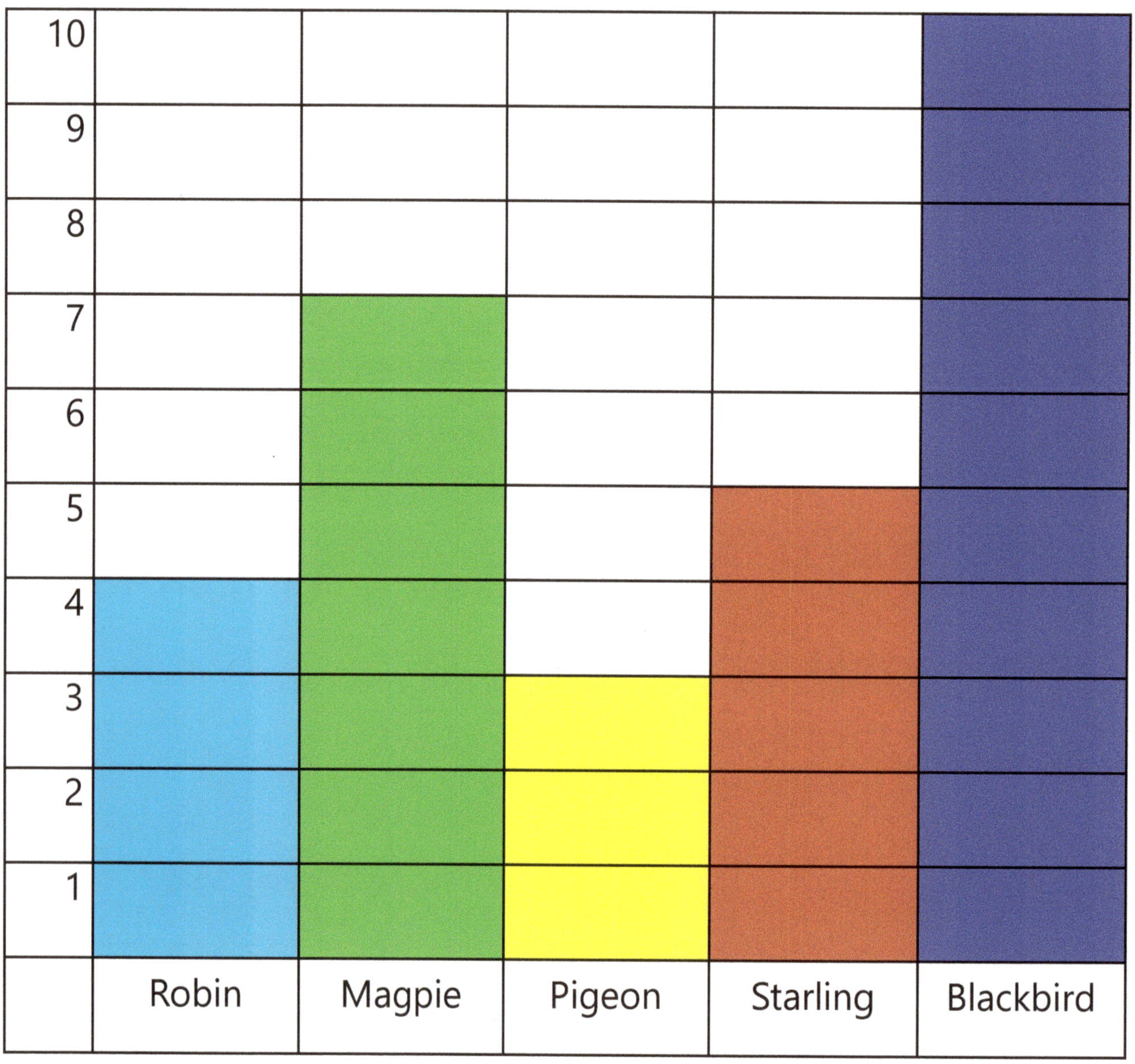

Planning a

News Report

Introduction *A leopard who has been terrorising jungle animals for years has finally been defeated… by a loris.*	**Event 1**	**Event 2**	**Event 3**
Event 4	**Event 5**	**Event 6**	**Eyewitness Quotes**

Ages 4+ Maths
Reading the Time

Learning Objective(s)

- To tell the time to the hour, and understand the hands on a clock face to show these times.
- To solve practical problems involving time.

Resources

- Copies of the "Don't Be Late!" worksheet from pages 38–39, enough for 1 per learner/ small group. Note that this worksheet should be double-sided.
- A teaching clock (optional – you can also use a whiteboard and marker / blackboard and chalk to demonstrate the hands on a clock face).
  You can also find teaching clocks online, e.g. at ***topmarks.co.uk/time/teaching-clock***
- Small class clocks (optional, but highly recommended).

Starter – *"Do Now!"*

Hooks into learning

Read/continue/re-read 'The REAL King of the Jungle' to the mark **<4+ M2>** (optional, but highly recommended).

Prior Knowledge Check

1. Using a teaching clock, or on the board, show midday.
2. Give your learners time to discuss the clock, and share what they know about clocks and time.
3. Then share ideas as a class. Discuss the clock: what it is for; the minute hand; the hour hand; how we know this clock shows 12 o'clock.
4. Let your learners know that 12 o'clock is also known as midday.
   If you didn't use the story as a starter for this lesson, you can take this opportunity to ask, "Who likes his lunch no later than midday?"
5. Let your learners know that you are all going to help the animals make sure they aren't late for Tenduay.

Main Input

1. Using small class clocks if you have them, look at how to make "o'clock" times using the minute hand and hour hand. Show how the minute hand points to the 12 every time, and the hour hand points to the hour. Spend time practising this.
2. Either individually, in pairs, or in groups, allow your learners to complete the clock faces on side one of the "Don't Be Late!" worksheet, showing the time at which each animal sets off to meet Tenduay.
3. When your learners have had ample time for this initial activity, bring them back together. On the teaching clock (or your board) show them 10 o'clock. Say,

   "If Elephant set off at 10 o'clock, how long did she have to travel to meet Tenduay?"

   Give your learners time to discuss this. If possible, hand out the small clocks to help them to explore.
4. Establish that each time the minute hand goes one full cycle around the clock, one hour has passed (show this on the teaching clock or your board). Then show them that from 10 to 12 o'clock, 2 hours have passed. Elephant had 2 hours to get to the meeting point.
5. Allow your learners to complete the second side of the worksheet. If possible, hand out the small clocks to help them. They will need to work out how long each animal has to get to the meeting place, given their starting time and the fact that they are required to be there by midday.

Plenary

- Continue to read 'The REAL King of the Jungle' to the mark **<4+ M3>** *OR* remind your learners that Loris was late.
- Set the following problem for your learners:

"Loris was late. She left at 2am and it took her 12 hours to get to the meeting place. At what time did she get there?"

- Allow your learners to work this out with a partner before sharing their thoughts as a class. Encourage them not just to give the answer, but to articulate how they worked the answer out.

Check In

Talk To Your Partner:

"What have you learnt today?"

Encourage your learners to share their thoughts. **We highly recommend this is the moment you share the Learning Objective with them, if at all.**

Don't Be Late!

Side 1 of 2

Show the time at which each animal sets off to meet Tenduay.

Antelope

10 o'clock

Gaur

4 o'clock

Red Panda

7 o'clock

Elephant

9 o'clock

Duck

8 o'clock

Monkey

11 o'clock

Loris

2 o'clock

Crocodile

5 o'clock

Python

7 o'clock

Don't Be Late!

Record how many hours each animal has got between their starting time and when they must meet Tenduay.

Animal	Start Time	Hours until 12 o'clock
Antelope	10 o'clock	
Gaur	4 o'clock	
Red Panda	7 o'clock	
Elephant	9 o'clock	
Duck	8 o'clock	
Monkey	11 o'clock	
Loris	2 o'clock	
Crocodile	5 o'clock	
Python	7 o'clock	

Ages 4+ Science
Reflective Materials

Learning Objective(s)

- To compare and group together a variety of everyday materials on the basis of their simple physical properties.
- To identify and compare the suitability of a variety of everyday materials.
- To work scientifically, including observing closely, performing simple tests, and using observations and ideas to suggest answers to questions.

Resources

- A large sheet (or circle) of blue paper.
- A range of reflective and non-reflective materials, e.g.:

  foil - cellophane - felt/fabric - newspaper - plastic mirror - shiny paper - tissue - coins
- Torches

Starter – *"Do Now!"*

Hooks into learning

1. Sit your learners on the floor in a circle around the large circle of blue paper. Let your learners know you're all going to imagine this is the cave that Loris lured Tenduay into, and the blue paper is the cave pool.
2. Spend time with your learners remembering what happened in the story. Pick a learner to be Loris and another to be Tenduay, and direct them with everyone's help to dramatise this moment in the story.
   You can also re-read this moment of the story if helpful, either before or during your learners' reconstruction.
3. At the point where Tenduay is supposed to see his reflection, stop the story. Ask the child who is playing Tenduay:

   "Can you see another leopard looking up at you from the pond?"

Prior Knowledge Check

Look into the pond yourself, which of course will not have a reflection. Act a little puzzled, then say:

"In the pond in the story, Tenduay saw his reflection. Why can't our Tenduay see his/her reflection in this pond?"

Spend some time discussing this, drawing out the fact that the water was reflective / had a reflective surface. Finish with:

"This paper pond is no good. If we are to have a pond that we can lure leopards into, we're going to need some reflective materials."

Main Input

1. Discuss what reflective means, i.e. "causing light to bounce away."
2. Spread out your range of materials. Ask your learners:
3. "How could we decide which materials are the most reflective?"
4. Share ideas, and establish that we need to shine a light onto the surfaces.

Independent/Group Activity

In pairs, children use a torch and the materials to investigate which materials are reflective and which are not.

Plenary

1. Invite your learners to use what they have found out to create a collaborative reflective pond using the best materials for the job.
2. Look at the finished pond together and talk about what they have found out.
3. If your learners have the appetite for it, have another go at recreating the end of the story!

Check In

Talk To Your Partner:

"What have you learnt today?"

Encourage your learners to share their thoughts. **We highly recommend this is the moment you share the Learning Objective with them, if at all.**

Story First

Ages 4+ English
Jungle News Report

Learning Objective(s)

- To develop an understanding of and proficiency with the sentence structure, text structure, punctuation, and terminology used for report writing.

Note that this lesson plan is designed to be spread across multiple lessons.

Resources

For each learner/pair/group, copies of...

- the 'News Report Writing Help Mat' (page 45)
- the 'News Report Model Text' (page 46)
- the 'News Report Writing Frame' (page 47)
- the 'News Report Planning Frame' (page 35 – optional)

For demonstrations, A3 copies of...

- the 'News Report Writing Frame' (page 47)
- the 'News Report Planning Frame' (page 35)
- some large sticky notes, or else large scraps of paper plus adhesive products

Starter – *"Do Now!"*

Hooks into learning

Show your learners your large copy of the 'News Report Writing Frame'. Give them time to read and discuss it.

- Do they know what a news report is?
- What features can they spot?

Spend some time looking at the 'News Report Model Text' and the 'News Report Writing Help Mat' to draw out some of the key features.

Main Input

1. Explain that you are all going to be Jungle Reporters:

"We need to tell the world what happened in the jungle the other day, when Loris saved his animal friends."

2. Discuss altogether the key events (e.g. "Tenduay ate the elephant"). Each time a key event is mentioned, write it on a large sticky note (or piece of scrap paper).
3. When you have sufficient events to write a report (you can decide how many you want, depending on your learners' writing level), sequence the pieces of paper together to form a plan using your large copy of the 'News Report Planning Frame'.
   You can either photocopy this plan for your learners to use, or have them copy it by hand into their own 'News Report Planning Frame' depending on their ability level(s).

Independent/Group Activity

When you have a plan, begin the following writing process over several lessons:

1. Model writing part of the News Report, adapting the teaching as required for your learners and their individual writing needs.
2. Allow your learners to write their part.
   Top Tip: *Allow your learners to write each chunk in their school writing books (or some scrap paper) to begin with, so that they can edit and improve as they go, before encouraging them to copy it up in their 'News Report Writing Frames'.*

Plenary

At the end of each writing session and/or at the start of the next one, share some good examples of writing your learners have done. Read the writing yourself, with enthusiasm, and correcting for minor spelling and grammar errors (you can speak with the learner about these afterwards).

With all your learners together, reflect upon what makes it effective writing. Support your learners to use the terminology they have been learning, spotting features relevant to writing a news report.

There's more...

Additional Ideas

Choose one or more of the following to enhance your learners enjoyment of this activity...

- Use drama to interview your learners in role as the jungle animals to get ideas, either about what happened, or how they felt about it. You could encourage your learners to use what they hear in these interviews as quotes in their reports.
- Your learners could watch an excerpt of a news reporter (e.g. *Newsround*) and, when they have written their report, they could record each other 'reading the news'.

Check In

Talk To Your Partner:

"What have you learnt today?"

Encourage your learners to share their thoughts. **We highly recommend this is the moment you share the Learning Objective with them, if at all.**

How to Write a News Report

Openers

First
Next
Then
A while later
Later that day
Finally

Conjunctions

and
so
but
because

Punctuation

ABC	capital letters
.	full stops
?	question marks
!	exclamation marks
“ ”	speech marks

Layout

Headline
Events organised into paragraphs

FOX GOBBLES GINGERBREAD MAN

22 February 2022

A gingerbread man has been gobbled up by a fox after escaping from its owners.

It all started when an old man and an old woman baked a gingerbread man.

First, the gingerbread man unexpectedly jumped out of the oven. He ran past the old woman and out of the door.

Next, the old man tried to catch him, but the gingerbread man was too fast and just kept on running.

After that, a horse galloped after the gingerbread man through a field, but even the horse was too slow.

Then a cow from a nearby farm joined in the chase. Once again, the gingerbread man outran them all.

Finally, the gingerbread man came to the river, and that was where he met his end.

It is believed that the fox tricked the gingerbread man into riding on his back before gobbling him up.

No trace of the gingerbread man has been found. The fox told us, "It was simply delicious."

The old woman was not very happy.

"I really wanted to eat that gingerbread man myself," she said.

TENDUAY DEFEATED!

A leopard who has been terrorising jungle animals for years has finally been defeated… by a loris.

Story First

Ages 4+ PSHE

Loris the Hero!

Learning Objective(s)

- To understand that we each have our own strengths, and ways we can help others.

Resources

- (On the board or printed) Images of a range of well-known superheroes, plus Loris – turn to page 50 for an image of Loris that you can photocopy.
- Paper (recommended A3) and art media.

Starter/Prior Knowledge Check – *"Do Now!"*

Hooks into learning

Give your learners time to discuss the superheroes as you go through them, sharing what they know and why they are heroes.

When you get to the slow loris, move on to the Main Input.

Main Input

1. Ask your learners...

"What makes Loris a hero?"

"Is he like the other heroes or not?"

Allow children time to share their opinions and ideas on this. Draw out the idea that Loris didn't have superpowers, but he did what he could to help.

2. Discuss with your learners...

"If Loris had a superpower, what could it be?"

Come up with one – e.g. "super clever", "super slow"...

3. Discuss how we can be everyday heroes, and the superpowers we might have. Give children time to talk about their own superpowers (e.g. super kind, super helpful, super writing), then gather a few ideas together on the board.

Independent Activity

Model this to your learners first, using Loris and/or yourself as an example.

1. Encourage your learners to draw themselves as a superhero, designing their own superhero clothing.
2. Ask each learner to create a speech bubble to go with their superhero character, stating what they can help with – e.g. "I am Super Loris and I can help you escape danger." (NB: Can be saved as a future activity.)

Plenary

1. Gather children on the carpet and invite them to share their superpowers and what they are good at.
2. Reflect on how we are all different and all have different superpowers, and how this is what makes the classroom an interesting and wonderful place to be.

Check In

Talk To Your Partner:

"What have you learnt today?"

Encourage your learners to share their thoughts. **We highly recommend this is the moment you share the Learning Objective with them, if at all.**

King Loris!

Ages 4+ Art
Indian Gond Art

Learning Objective(s)

- To use a range of materials creatively.
- To use drawing to develop and share ideas.
- To develop art and design techniques in using colour, pattern, texture, line.
- To discover the art and practices of the Indian Gond tradition.

Resources

- A slideshow presentation of Gond art. Find appropriate images online by searching for 'Indian Gond art', or scan the images included here on pages 51, 54, and 55
- Paper, pencils, and fine tip colouring pens
- Photocopies of the animal outlines from pages 56–57 (optional)

Preparation

You may wish to read up on the origins of Gond art in order to share these with your learners.

Prior Knowledge Check

Ask your learners,

"In which country would we find the jungle of Tenduay and Loris?"

Starter – *"Do Now!"*

Hooks into learning

1. Show your Gond slideshow presentation to your learners, inviting them to look at and discuss the images.

"What do you like about these images?"

"Is there anything you don't like about them?"

"Which piece of art is your favourite, and why?"

Main Input

1. Let your learners know that all of this artwork is in the same style, known as 'Gond' because it was started by the Gond tribe of people in India.
2. Using the images side by side, ask your learners to spot the similarities...

   "Can we work out what makes this a piece of Gond art work?"

   Draw out the themes, i.e. **nature, dot and dash patterns.**
3. Let your learners know that, because the story of 'The REAL King of the Jungle' is from India, you're all going to try to use this Indian artistic style to create pictures of the animals from the story.
4. Model to your learners how to create an animal outline for one of the animals in the story (or use one of the outlines we have provided for you), then filling it with patterns in the Gond style, using pencil first and then going over and/or filling it in using fine felt tip pens.

Independent/Group Activity

Allow your learners to create their own Gond artworks, either creating their own outlines or using copies of the outlines provided for you in this book.

Plenary

- Bring your learners back together and revisit the key elements of Indian Gond artwork that you all discovered earlier. Select one learner's artwork and model positive reflection on their use of Gond techniques.
- Put your learners in pairs to reflect on each other's artwork, encouraging them to explore how they managed to include the key features of Gond techniques.

Check In

Talk To Your Partner:

"What have you learnt today?"

Encourage your learners to share their thoughts. **We highly recommend this is the moment you share the Learning Objective with them, if at all.**

Gond Loris

Gond Tenduay

Lesson First

Ages 7+ Music
Jungle Drumming

Learning Objective(s)

- To compose a piece of music using your voice.

Resources

- Paper and pens.
- Recording software and devices (optional).

Starter – *"Do Now!"*

Hooks into learning

Ask your learners:

"What sounds could we hear in the jungle? Create a list of them."

Main Input

1. Encourage your learners to spend a few minutes recreating some of these sounds in small groups using only their voices.
2. Ask your learners:

"What would happen if we made one of these sounds more than once, exactly the same way each time? Could we get a rhythm?"

Model a demonstration, and/or invite a group to be an example.

If possible, model how to record one of these sounds into recording software and play it back, then model how to create several instances of the sound to make a repeating pattern.

3. Ask your learners:

"How would the sound change if we played more than one of these repeating patterns at the same time?"

Invite a group to be an example, assisting in the demonstration as necessary.

Again, if possible, record one or two further sounds and then model how to layer the patterns to create a multitrack sound file.

Independent/Group Activity

Allow your learners to create their own compositions in small groups, and/or create recordings of their compositions if possible.

If you have the ability to let them record, this activity can also be attempted by learners working individually.

Plenary

Choose one or more of the following...

- Invite your learners to create vocals to go over the top of their compositions.
- Ask your learners to think of ways that they could notate their compositions.

Check In

Talk To Your Partner:

"What have you learnt today?"

Encourage your learners to share their thoughts. **We highly recommend this is the moment you share the Learning Objective with them, if at all.**

Ages 7+ Maths

Inches and Centimetres

Learning Objective(s)

- To convert between inches and centimetres.

Resources

- A selection of straws of different lengths.
  If you plan to try the Plenary, you will need enough for at least one straw per learner.
- A selection of rulers displaying inches and/or centimetres. For the purposes of this lesson, it is most ideal if the rulers display just one unit of measurement, e.g. inches.
- Paper and pens.

Preparation

If you wish to try the Plenary: Note the lengths of your 9 shortest straws in both inches and centimetres, then mix them up with the rest of your collection.

Prior Knowledge Check

Talk To Your Partner:

"What different units of measurement can you think of?"

Encourage your learners to share what they know.

Starter – *"Do Now!"*

Hooks into learning

1. Read/continue/re-read 'The REAL King of the Jungle' to the mark **<7+ M1>** (optional, but highly recommended).
2. Talk To Your Partner:

"What units could the animals use to measure their straws?"

"Where else do we find these units being used?"

After each question, encourage your learners to share what they know.
If none of your learners suggest inches or centimetres, ask:

"Has anyone heard of the imperial/metric system?"

Main Input

1. Let your learners know that the animals will be measuring using the imperial system, which uses inches – but most countries today use the metric system, which uses centimetres.
2. Let your learners know there are 2.54cm in 1″, then ask:

"How many centimetres in two inches? four? seven?"

(Optional) For each challenge, allow them to work with each other in teams to find the solutions using pencils and paper within a reasonably short time limit. The ***losers*** of the first challenge get to use calculators for the next. The ***winners*** of the third challenge have their calculators and/or pens and paper taken away...

Independent/Group Activity

Pass each learner or small group a selection of straws and rulers, and challenge them to measure them all in inches/centimetres and then convert them into centimetres/inches.

This activity will challenge your learners more (and therefore be more beneficial) if the rulers don't show both units of measurement. If you can only access dual-unit rulers, perhaps cover one set of units with strong opaque sticky tape, go over them using a permanent marker pen, or (if the markings are raised) remove them with sandpaper.

Plenary

Reward your learners' hard work by continuing the story, and use their answers to work out which learner is which animal. For example...

1. Collect all the straws, then hand out one to each learner at random.
   Make sure your 9 shortest straws are among them.
2. Let them know the length of the shortest straw in centimetres. They will need to convert from inches to confirm that they've got the right one.
3. Ask the possessor of that straw to show that they are Gaur, the first animal to be eaten, in whatever manner they wish (e.g. pose, acting, sound effect).
4. Repeat the process for the 8 other animals chosen by straws.

Check In

Talk To Your Partner:

"What have you learnt today?"

Encourage your learners to share their thoughts. **We highly recommend this is the moment you share the Learning Objective with them, if at all.**

Story First

Ages 7+ PSHE

Ecology

Learning Objective(s)

- To understand an individual's role in relation to others and the environment.

Resources

- Paper and writing/drawing materials.
- Craft materials (optional).

Starter – *"Do Now!"*

Hooks into learning

Ask your learners:

"What do you think 'ecology' might mean?"

Main Input

1. Let your learners know:

"Ecology is the world we use when thinking about how individuals and the environment affect each other."

2. Discuss with your learners how this relates to the story of 'The REAL King of the Jungle'.

What does the jungle look like when Tenduay is eating indiscriminately?

What does it look like after the animals come up with their offer?

What does it look like after Tenduay has gone?

Is any one of these pictures perfect?

How do we affect the ecology of *our* area? And how does it affect us?

What can we do to either promote or prevent these actions?

Independent/Group Activity

Choose one or more of the following...

- Invite your learners to create images/models to show the ecology of the jungle at one or more stages of the story.
- Invite your learners to create images/models to show what the jungle would look like with a 'perfect' ecological balance.
- Invite your learners to produce posters promoting actions which benefit their local ecosystem, or preventing actions which damage it.
  This last activity can also be undertaken with your learners imagining themselves to be part of any other ecosystem, including Loris and Tenduay's jungle.

Check In

Talk To Your Partner:

"What have you learnt today?"

Encourage your learners to share their thoughts. **We highly recommend this is the moment you share the Learning Objective with them, if at all.**

Story First

Ages 7+ English

Adjective Hunter

Learning Objective(s)

- To collect a range of adjectives.

Resources

- One or more of the animal feature cards from pages 23–29.
- Photocopies of pages from 'The REAL King of the Jungle', enough for at least one page per learner.
- Highlighter pens.
- Pens and paper.

Starter – *"Do Now!"*

Hooks into learning

Show one of the feature cards and ask your learners:

"What could this animal be doing? Write a sentence using a verb to show what the animal could be doing."

Take answers and explore more powerful verbs. Repeat with other feature cards if desired.

Prior Knowledge Check

Talk To Your Partner:

"Today we will build up a bank of adjectives. What is an adjective?"

Encourage your learners to share what they remember.

Main Input

1. Ask your learners for some examples of adjectives and write them somewhere visible for everyone to see (e.g. on a whiteboard, or large sheet of paper).
2. Let your learners know:

"We are going to look for adjectives in the story of 'The REAL King of the Jungle'."

3. Read the first two pages together and discuss any adjectives in this section, writing them on your visible space too.

Independent/Group Activity

1. Invite your learners to read the remaining pages of the story, either individually, in pairs, or in small groups, and highlight them as they go using the highlighter pens.
2. After leaving a reasonable amount of time, begin collecting the adjectives found.
   If any adverbs highlighted, add them, but in a separate part of the board – see Plenary.

Plenary

Choose one or more of the following...

- Discuss the definition of an adverb, and how it is different to an adjective.
- Expand their sentences from the Starter using adjectives and/or adverbs.
- Spend some time talking about their favourite adjectives/adverbs, and why.
  Allow this to include aural delight, i.e. just the sound of the word, or even visual delight, i.e. how the word looks on the page. This can lead to discussions around onomatopoeia, unique spellings, etc.

Check In

Talk To Your Partner:

"What have you learnt today?"

Encourage your learners to share their thoughts. **We highly recommend this is the moment you share the Learning Objective with them, if at all.**

The Farmer and the Boggart

Based on a Lincolnshire folk tale
Adapted and written by Chip Colquhoun
Illustrated by Mario Coelho

When Farmer Rob arrived at the village of Mumby, he knew straight away that something was wrong.

At the start of the day, he had been in the English seaside town of Skegness, which was full of people playing, laughing, and holding hands. But although he was still in the flat, green, grassy fields of England, the village of Mumby felt like an alien desert.

For starters, the streets were empty and quiet – even though it was daytime. All the shops had signs on their doors saying "CLOSED", and there weren't even any birds in the sky.

<4+ G1>

Rob went to the pub. Pubs were always good places to go for news. Rob thought he might find out what was wrong if he went in there.

Plus, he had been walking for a long time – and pubs were good places to drink, too!

But while the sign on the pub door said "OPEN", there didn't seem to be anyone in. Rob went to the counter and rang the bell.

A short man poked his head through a door between the shelves full of bottles. He looked as if he was expecting a ghost. "Huh... hullo?"

Farmer Rob asked for a drink.

The man came out warily, taking two little steps at a time. He wore an apron, which showed that he was the owner of the pub. "We have a little beer left," he said, "but not very much. We're out of wine. You can have some water, but not too much. I need to make sure I have enough to clean my baby tonight, or she'll get sick."

Farmer Rob frowned. It was very unusual for a pub to have so little to drink. He asked if there was anything to eat.

The landlord shook his head. "Sorry. There's only one potato left in the whole house, and that has to feed my family for the rest of the week:

me, my wife, our two little girls, and the baby."

Now Rob was shocked. A pub with little to drink, and no food? Not even any snacks?

And a potato to feed the whole family? *One potato?*

<4+ M1>

Rob demanded to know what was going on.

The pub owner opened his mouth to answer, but suddenly stopped. After a worried sigh, he said, "It's the land. The land just isn't kind to farmers. All the farmers who come here have so much trouble with the land that they go away, so we only get food when someone comes by with food to sell – and they don't come very often."

Farmer Rob wondered why the people didn't leave Mumby and go somewhere else.

"We're too hungry and thirsty," the pub owner replied, "so we don't have the energy to do anything."

Rob couldn't believe it. Land that wasn't kind to farmers? He had never heard anything so strange in all his life.

But of course, Farmer Rob was a farmer. Perhaps he could help.

Still the pub landlord looked sad. "I don't think you'll have much better luck," he told Rob, "but thank you for wanting to help. If you try, I expect you'll be gone by tomorrow."

Farmer Rob didn't think so. He really wanted to help, and he was sure that he could. After all, he had left his home in Skegness to start a farm somewhere in the country. Here in Mumby, it seemed they really needed someone like him.

So Rob left the pub and went into the nearest field. It wasn't long before he discovered what the *real* problem was.

As soon as Rob stepped into the field, the ground in front of him began to shake... Then it began to swirl... Then it *exploded* in a big burst of mud!

And there, standing in front of Rob and staring at him with a wide ugly smirk, was a *boggart.*

Farmer Rob knew it was a boggart because his grandma had once told him what boggarts looked like: large men bent forward so they were almost the shape and size of a cow, with extra-long arms that dangled to the ground, and hair as thick as string. Also, a boggart's mouth was just a bit too big, and its eyes a bit too round – and it would never ever blink.

<4+ E1>

The Farmers Arms PUB

That description was a perfect match for the creature that now stood in front of Rob. And *that* meant Rob also now understood why the pub landlord hadn't said anything about the boggart: Rob's grandma had told him that if anyone ever spoke about a boggart, that boggart would come to steal their children at night.

The boggart's voice sounded a little like a piece of metal dragging across a stone. "This is my land, farmer! I will let you work on it, but only if you give me everything you grow: your food, your animals, and even your children..."

Yep. It was definitely a boggart. Rob's grandma had said boggarts liked to make deals like that: horrible deals that had probably scared the other farmers away. No farmer would want to work hard on a farm only to give all their food and animals to a boggart – and they certainly wouldn't like the idea of a boggart taking their children.

But Rob's grandma had also given him two very important pieces of advice for dealing with boggarts. Advice Number One was, *Boggarts will always try to make a deal –* ***especially*** *if they think it's better for them.*

And Advice Number Two was—

Oh, wait – I don't have timc to tell you that, because Farmer Rob was already asking the boggart if anyone had ever accepted its deal before.

"Never!" the boggart replied, and then laughed wickedly.

Farmer Rob then asked if the boggart grew his own food and animals.

The boggart stopped laughing. "No," it said angrily. "I have to steal the food they have in the village – and they don't have much left. And when I get hungry, I have to eat worms."

So Farmer Rob suggested a new deal: he would farm the land if the boggart allowed him to keep *half* of the food and the animals and his children. That way the boggart would still get plenty to eat, but Farmer Rob wouldn't want to run away.

The boggart hummed as it thought — a hum that sounded like a wasp trapped in a metal bucket. Then it asked, "You would accept this deal then? You get only half of the food and the animals and your children for yourself?"

Rob explained that he wasn't going to keep all the food for himself. He wanted to share it with the village.

That was even better for the boggart, of course: it meant there would be more food in the village to steal!

So the boggart smiled nastily. "I'm liking the sound of this," it said. "Yes, I will only take half, so you stay and make more."

Rob then asked the boggart whether it wanted the half of the food from above the ground, or the half from below the ground.

The boggart hummed again, that gritty waspish sound, then said, "How do you make the food?"

Farmer Rob explained that he would plant some seeds into the ground.

"Then I'll take the half below the ground! That's bound to be the best bit..." the boggart declared, then gave another wicked laugh. Before Rob could say anything else, it added, "*Deal!* Ha!"

And it grinned wide enough for Rob to see its dark green teeth dripping with oily spit.

Now, would you like to know Grandma's Advice Number Two on the subject of boggarts? Well—

Oh, wait – I don't have time to tell you that right now, because Farmer Rob had already taken some seeds from his bag, got hold of a spade, and set to work.

First, he worked his back hard, digging lots of long straight lines all across the field – while the boggart watched and drooled, thinking about all the food it would eat.

Next, Farmer Rob worked his legs hard, walking up and down to drop the seeds into the long straight lines he'd dug – while the boggart watched and licked its lips, thinking about how luscious all that food would taste.

Then, Farmer Rob worked his hands hard, using a shovel to cover all the seeds with soil — while the boggart watched and cackled, thinking about how big its muscles would get after eating all that food.

Finally, Farmer Rob worked his shoulders hard, carrying bucket after bucket of water from the river to pour over the field – while the boggart watched and rubbed its hands with glee, thinking about how all that food would soon be in its belly.

At last, Farmer Rob sat down beside the field for a rest.

The boggart snarled. "Hey! You can't rest! You have to make our food!"

Farmer Rob explained that they now had to wait a while for the seeds to grow.

"Wait a while?" the boggart asked. "How long?"

Rob said that it usually took four or five months.

"Four or five months?!" the boggart screeched.

Well. While we wait, would you like to know Grandma's Advice Number Two on the subject of boggarts? Well—

Oh, wait – I don't have time to tell you that right now, because the boggart decided it wasn't going to wait for the seeds to grow naturally. Instead, it held its hands over the field, and said, *"Acceleration germination!"*

In less than a minute, all the seeds grew into hundreds of tall, gleaming green plants, each with several succulent peapods dangling from its branches.

A boggart's eyes are already extra wide, but now *this* boggart's eyes were *extra* extra wide! It slurped up its own drool just thinking about the tasty plump peas inside those peapods!

<4+ MU1>

But Farmer Rob quickly stepped forward and reminded the boggart about their deal: he would take the half above the ground, and the boggart would take the half below the ground.

"Fine," the boggart said, "but hurry up! We haven't got all story!"

Farmer Rob told the boggart it would go a little quicker if he had some help from the village, and ran back to knock on people's doors. He soon returned with at least one person from every house in Mumby, including the pub landlord, the landlord's wife, their two daughters, and their baby. Almost every grown-up was pushing a wheelbarrow.

Then Rob took hold of the long, curvy blade known as a scythe, and began slicing the stalks of the peapods. The villagers of Mumby filled their wheelbarrows with those peapods, took them off home, then came back again for more. They did this again and again and again, each time pushing a pile of plump and juicy peapods.

<7+ M1>

It was hard work, but most of them felt more pain in their faces than in their legs or arms – they were all smiling for the first time in ages!

As soon as Rob had finished, and the last villager wheeled their barrow away, the boggart grabbed the spade and greedily began digging for its own half.

But all that peapods leave under the ground are slithery roots. Those are as thin as worms – and ten times as chewy.

The boggart's skin turned a fiery red. It could have eaten worms *without* Farmer Rob's help! It whirled around to face Farmer Rob and screeched, *"You tricked me!"*

Farmer Rob looked confused. After all, they'd made a deal.

"But you took the good half!" the boggart screamed. "I think I'll eat *you* for dinner tonight...!"

Farmer Rob held up his hands, and pointed out that the boggart had learned a valuable lesson: when you harvest a farm, you should always make sure you get the good half.

"What use is the lesson if I don't have any food?!" the boggart cried.

Farmer Rob pulled another packet of seeds from his bag, and offered to let the boggart have the half from *above* the ground this time.

"Deal!" the boggart spat quickly. Then, once again, it sat back to watch Farmer Rob do all the hard work.

First, Farmer Rob worked his back hard, digging lots of long straight furrows all across the field.

Next, Farmer Rob worked his legs hard, walking up and down to drop the seeds into the furrows.

Then, Farmer Rob worked his hands hard, using a shovel to cover all the seeds with soil.

Finally, Farmer Rob worked his shoulders hard, carrying pail after pail of water from the river to pour over the field.

At last, Farmer Rob lay down beside the field for a rest.

While he rests, would you like to know Grandma's Advice Number Two on the subject of boggarts? Well—

Oh, wait – I don't have time to tell you that right now, because the boggart had once again decided it wouldn't wait for the seeds to grow naturally. Instead, it once again held its hands over the field, and said, *"Acceleration germination!"*

In less than a minute, all the seeds grew into hundreds of bushy bundles of bright green leaves.

The boggart's skin was its normal colour now, and its eyes went back to being stupendously wide. It quickly stepped forward, reminding Farmer Rob about their new deal: the boggart would harvest the half above the ground, and Farmer Rob would harvest the half below the ground.

The boggart rubbed its hands together, then waved them at the scythe.

Farmer Rob watched in amazement as the scythe quickly cut all the leaves, without the boggart having to do a single ounce of hard work.

Then the boggart sat beside the field, ready to munch on its feast of thick and juicy leaves, while the villagers returned with their wheelbarrows to collect the roots from under the ground.

Those roots turned out to be potatoes. Farmer Rob dug them out with his spade, and the villagers of Mumby piled them into their wheelbarrows, ferrying them off to their homes and back, again and again, each time heaving a heavy harvest of potatoes.

It was tough work, but most of them felt more pain in their bellies than in their legs or arms – because they were laughing with delight for the first time in ages.

Meanwhile, the boggart took a huge mouthful of its leaves...

...and instantly felt sick! It quickly spat the leaves out, then rolled on the ground and clutched its aching stomach.

Farmer Rob came over and told the boggart that it probably shouldn't eat those leaves. After all, potato leaves are poisonous.

The boggart turned red with rage again, ready to rip Rob apart from eyelid to toenail...

...but it was also ill from the potato leaves, so it could only sit and groan. It began to wonder how it could get its own back on Farmer Rob.

Oo! While the boggart wonders what to do, would you like to know Grandma's Advice Number Two on the subject of boggarts? Well...

The Farmers Arms
PUB

Oh, wait. I don't have time to tell you that right now, because the boggart didn't take that long to think. It said, "Alright, you've had your fun. But it ends now! I'm going away to rest – but while I'm gone, you need to plant another field full of food. I'll come back in the morning to make it grow, and then I'll take all the food from the *left* side – above *and* below! And if you share any of your side with the villagers, I'll steal it from them!"

Before Farmer Rob could say anything, the boggart added, "*Deal!* Deal deal *deal!* And if you *don't* plant the field ready for tomorrow... I'll eat *you* instead!"

Farmer Rob didn't like the idea of getting eaten. So as soon as the boggart had vanished into its home in the mud, Rob quickly set to work planting some more seeds.

First, Farmer Rob worked his back hard, digging lots of long straight furrows all across the field. He also made sure he picked up all the stones he found on the right side, and put them in a pile.

Next, Farmer Rob worked his legs hard, walking up and down to drop the seeds into the furrows. He also made sure he dropped all the stones from the right side into the left side.

Then, Farmer Rob worked his hands hard, using a shovel to cover all the seeds with soil. He made sure that he covered the stones on the left side too.

Finally, Farmer Rob worked his shoulders hard, carrying pail after pail from the river to water the field. He made sure to give the same amount of water to both sides – after all, fair is fair.

At last, Farmer Rob lay down beside the field to sleep. He hadn't even had time to find a house in Mumby yet.

Now I know this may seem like the best time for me to tell you Grandma's Advice Number Two on the subject of boggarts, but here's the thing: Rob had worked so long and hard to make sure he didn't get eaten, he had worked all through the night – so a cock was already cock-a-doodle-dooing to announce the morning, and the boggart reappeared!

"Right!" the boggart shrieked. Its skin was still red, but it no longer looked ill. "I'm going to harvest my half *first* this time!"

Farmer Rob was too sleepy to argue.

The boggart turned to the field, held up its hands, and howled, *"Acceleration germination!"*

In less than a minute, all the seeds grew into hundreds of thick fat wads of creamy cauliflowers, cradled by thick leaves that held them close to the ground.

The boggart quickly reminded Farmer Rob about their new deal: the boggart would take the half on the left, above *and* below the ground.

Then the boggart rubbed its hands together, and gestured towards the scythe. Once again, Farmer Rob watched in astonishment as the scythe began reaping the cauliflowers...

...but instead of reaping them quickly, like it had with the potato leaves, the scythe began to struggle. You see, to reap the cauliflowers, it had to cut quite close to the ground — and it kept hitting stones.

So many stones, in fact, that the blade soon became blunt, and could hardly cut at all!

The boggart couldn't believe it. The boggart began to wail angrily — one long cry that sounded like a hundred babies crying, a thousand nails scraping down a chalkboard, a hundred thousand shoes shuffling across a carpet, and a million cats coughing up hairballs *all at once*.

And its skin got redder and brighter and hotter and bigger until it *burst into flame!*

The Farmers Arms PUB

Farmer Rob watched the boggart disappear into a fireball, and the fireball disappear into the wind – and he enjoyed a little smile. Now the boggart would never trouble the village of Mumby again. Soon he'd be able to sharpen the scythe to harvest his side of the field, which would give him more than enough cauliflower to share with the villagers.

But not right now. After all that hard work, he deserved a bit of a nap.

Oo! Now the story's over, would you like to know Grandma's Advice Number Two on the subject of boggarts?

Well, you've probably worked it out by now: boggarts are not at all clever – and if you can trick them into a rage, they'll explode in a big ball of fire, and they'll never bother you again...

'FARMER AND BOGGART' LESSON PLANS

Story Pause

Ages 4+ Geography and DT
Villages like Mumby

Learning Objective(s)

- To use basic geographical vocabulary to refer to key physical and human features.
- To devise a simple map.
- To create a simple 3D map using the flange method.

Resources

- A large piece of paper (the base of your map).
- Cut out copies of the Village Feature cards on pages 82–83.
- Plain card and colouring pens/pencils.
- Scissors.
- Glue or sticky tape.

Preparation

- Prepare the base of your map by drawing out some basic 2D features in advance, such as fields, rivers, ponds, and roads.

  You can use the Lincolnshire village of Mumby as a guide, or you can create your own fictional village and call it Mumby for the purposes of this lesson.

Starter – *"Do Now!"*

Hooks into learning

1. Read/continue/re-read 'The Farmer and the Boggart' to the mark **<4+ G1>** (optional, but highly recommended).
2. Lay out the base of your map, and model making a 'Village of Mumby' sign using the flange method (see page 84). Attach the sign to your map.

Main Input

1. Ask your learners:

"If this were the village of Mumby, what other geographical features could we add to it?"

2. Share some initial ideas if required, using the Feature cards, placing each in turn on your map. If your learners mention any features shown on the cards, reveal these and place them onto your map also.
3. If your learners mention features that are from towns or cities, take the opportunity to discuss this with them, pointing out that towns and cities have some additional and/or different geographical features to villages.
4. Introduce them to any other geographical features that have not yet been mentioned, using any remaining Feature cards.
5. Model again how to create some 3D geographical features using the flange method to stand them up.

Independent/Group Activity

Invite your learners to create their own 3D features to attach to the map using the flange method, either individually or in small groups.

Plenary

1. Display the map in the middle of your learners.
2. Go through the features of a village again, this time asking your learners to point them out on your map as you do.
3. Reward your learners for their work in this lesson by continuing to read the story!

Check In

Talk To Your Partner:

"What have you learnt today?"

Encourage your learners to share their thoughts. **We highly recommend this is the moment you share the Learning Objective with them, if at all.**

Village Feature Cards

Village Feature Cards

Flange Method

1. After you have drawn an image on your sheet of card, cut several short lines of equal length up from the bottom end. This will create 'tabs' or 'feet'.
   We recommend a minimum of three lines (four or more feet) for stability.
2. Fold out the feet in alternate directions.
3. Stick the feet to your base using glue or sticky tape.

1.

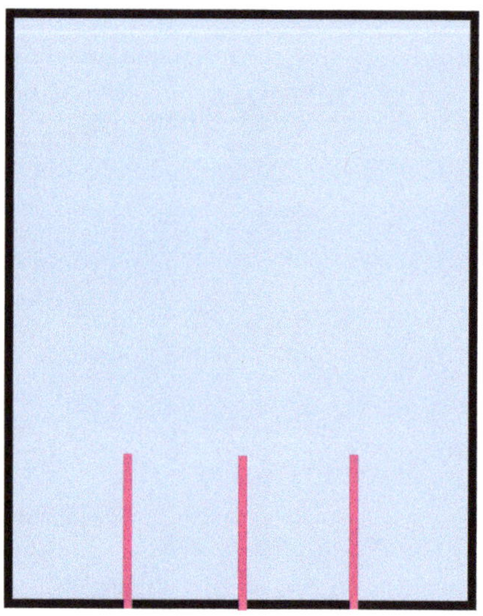

2.

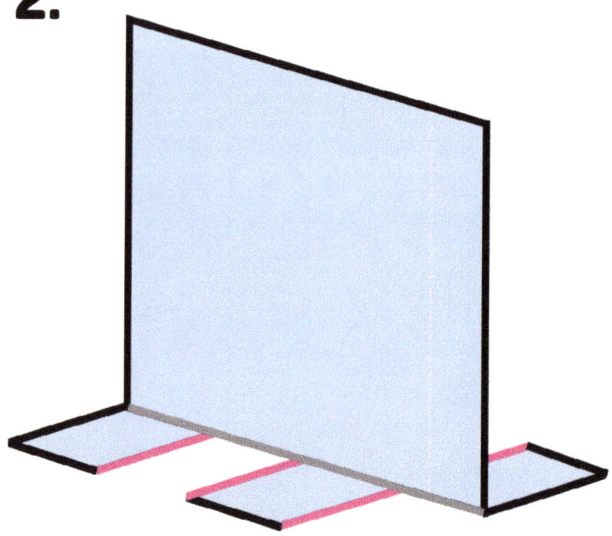

Paper Potatoes

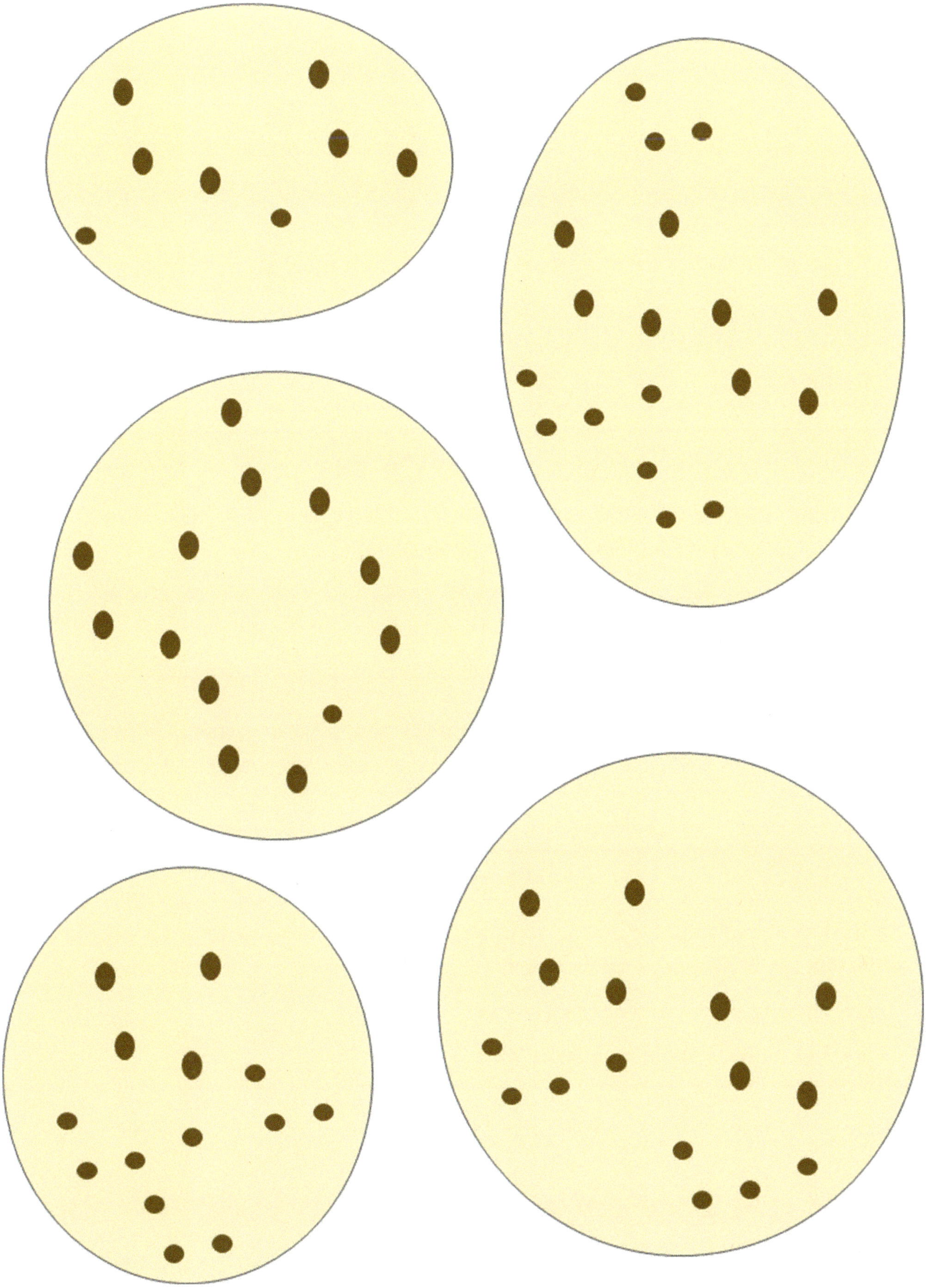

Story Pause

Ages 4+ Maths

Quarters of a Potato

Learning Objective(s)

- To recognise, find, and name a half as one of two equal parts of an object, shape or quantity.
- To recognise, find, and name a quarter as one of four equal parts of an object, shape or quantity.
- To recognise, find, name, and write fractions of a length, shape, set of objects, or quantity.

Resources

- Multiple copies of the potatoes from page 85, enough for at least 3 per learner/small group (plus yourself for the Plenary preparation).
- Copies of the potato worksheet on page 89, enough for 1 per learner/small group.
- Scissors for each learner/small group.
- Glue and/or sticky tape.
- Optional: Depending on the abilities of your learners, you can exchange the paper potatoes at any point in this lesson for potatoes made from putty/playdough/modelling clay.

Preparation

For the Plenary, attempt the potato worksheet yourself, but have some that are correct and some that are deliberately incorrect, such as...

- one showing ¾ but with unequal pieces
- another showing ½ but notated as ¼

Starter – *"Do Now!"*

Hooks into learning

1. Read/continue/re-read 'The Farmer and the Boggart' to the mark **<4+ M1>** (optional, but highly recommended).
2. Present your learners with a paper potato, and ask:

"If you and three other friends had only this potato to eat, how could you share it equally?"

3. Give your learners time to think about this, and give out paper potatoes for them to explore with (ideally one between four, or else one between two).
4. The aim at this point is not to tell them or model to them what to do, but to give them time to try out ideas. They may fold the potato or cut it. Even if they are along the wrong lines (e.g. the pieces are unequal), at this point just let them try things out – albeit with your support, perhaps dropping in ideas. For example, if they have made unequal pieces, you might say,

"I can see you've got four pieces there, but which piece would you rather have?"

5. If any learners finish quickly, give them another paper potato of a different size or shape to experiment with.

Main Input

1. Bring your learners back together and invite them to discuss what they found out.
2. During this discussion, draw out the fact that the pieces need to be equal, and model how to do this – i.e. fold a potato into half, then fold it in half again.
3. Show your learners that there are four equal pieces, and explain that each piece is called a quarter. Have them repeat these key phrases.
4. Show what ¼ looks like when written on a display board, and demonstrate writing this on each piece of your potato.
5. Show your learners three pieces of the four, then say:

"What if I was feeling greedy and ate 3 of the pieces? I would have eaten three quarters of the potato, three out of the four pieces."

6. Show your learners what the fraction ¾ looks like when written.

There's more...

Independent/Group Activity

Distribute the paper potatoes and worksheets among your learners (either individually or in small groups), and invite them to:

1. cut/fold each potato into quarters;
2. stick the quarters onto their worksheet and label them as ¼ each; then finally
3. colour either ¼ or ¾ of each potato, writing next to it the fraction they have coloured.

You may wish to model an example first, and/or then circulate and support as needed.

OPTIONAL: Introduce your learners to the fact that two quarters is equal to one half, then encourage them to find and label ½ of a paper potato.

Plenary

1. Bring your learners back together, then invite them to assess and mark ***your*** completed worksheet. Have you found ¼ or ¾? If not, why?
2. Reward your learners for their work in this lesson by continuing to read the story!

Check In

Talk To Your Partner:

"What have you learnt today?"

Encourage your learners to share their thoughts. **We highly recommend this is the moment you share the Learning Objective with them, if at all.**

Sharing the Potato

The villagers of Mumby need your help to share the potatoes!

1. Take one potato at a time.
2. Fold or cut it into quarters.
3. Colour ¼ of the potato, or ¾ of the potato.
4. Glue it into this sheet.
5. Write beside it either ¼ or ¾.

Ages 4+ English

Look Out, Boggart About!

Learning Objective(s)

- To develop positive attitudes and stamina for writing by writing for different purposes.

Resources

- One large copy of the 'Description of a Boggart' on page 92, and/or multiple copies to distribute among your learners.
- One large copy of the 'Boggart Writing Help Mat' on page 93, and/or multiple copies to distribute among your learners.
- Paper and pens/pencils.

Preparation

- Prepare one sheet of paper in advance with a title in large letters reading,

Welcome to Mumby... but watch out for the boggart!

Starter – *"Do Now!"*

Hooks into learning

1. Read/continue/re-read 'The Farmer and the Boggart' to the mark **<4+ E1>** (optional, but highly recommended).
   IMPORTANT: If using the Story Pause method, ideally your learners won't have seen the illustration on page 68 yet, so try to keep it from them.
2. Say:

"That creature seems a little scary, doesn't it! Maybe the village should have a sign to warn people..."

Main Input

1. Let your learners see your sign-so-far (which should be blank but for the title in large letters), and invite them into a discussion about what else should be on the sign.
2. Draw out or suggest the ideas that the sign should have a picture of the boggart, and a description, then suggest to your learners that you could all create the sign with help from the **adjectives** in the story.
3. Use your copy or copies of the 'Boggart Descriptions' to find adjectives and transfer them to the Adjective frame on the 'Boggart Writing Mat'.

Independent/Group Activity

1. Invite your learners to begin by drawing a boggart based on the descriptions found, either individually or in small groups.
2. After a reasonable amount of time, model writing a description of the boggart's appearance at an appropriate the level for your learners, using adjectives, expanded noun phrases, effective punctuation, etc. Model use of the 'Boggart Writing Help Mat' as a guide.
3. Encourage your learners to prepare their own descriptions on rough paper/in writing books first, then copy them out onto their warning signs.

Plenary

Choose one or more of the following...

- With everyone together at the end (and/or optionally at various points throughout the Independent/Group Activity): share the work of one or more learners and encourage comments from the others about what the learner has done really well in their writing. For example:

"Can you spot some good adjectives?"

"Can you see any effective punctuation?"

"What do you think is the best sentence in this piece of writing? Why do you think it's good?"

- Reward your learners for their work in this lesson by continuing to read the story!

Check In

Talk To Your Partner:

"What have you learnt today?"

Encourage your learners to share their thoughts. **We highly recommend this is the moment you share the Learning Objective with them, if at all.**

Description of a Boggart

There, standing in front of Rob and staring at him with a wide ugly smirk, was a *boggart*.

Farmer Rob knew it was a boggart because his grandma had once told him what boggarts looked like: large men bent forward so they were almost the shape and size of a cow, with extra-long arms that dangled to the ground, and hair as thick as string. Also, a boggart's mouth was just a bit too big, and its eyes a bit too round – and it would never ever blink.

It grinned wide enough for Rob to see its dark green teeth dripping with oily spit.

How to Describe a Boggart

Openers

He has
He is
His
On his

Conjunctions

and
with
which
that

Punctuation

ABC	capital letters
.	full stops
,	commas (to separate items in a list)
!	exclamation marks

Adjectives

Story Pause

Ages 4+ Music

A Sound Story

Learning Objective(s)

- To play tuned and untuned instruments musically.
- To experiment with, create, select, and combine sounds

Resources

- The short version of 'The Farmer and the Boggart', found on page 96.
- Copies of the 'Boggart Sound Effects List' on page 97, cut up and separated so each effect is on its own slip of paper.
- For 9+ learners, you only need enough effects to provide one per learner or small group.
- For 8 learners or fewer, you only need one of each effect (some learners/small groups will have multiple).
- A range of untuned percussion instruments – and/or anything else useful and noisy you might have laying around...!

Starter – *"Do Now!"*

Hooks into learning

Read/continue/re-read 'The Farmer and the Boggart' to the mark **<4+ MU1>** (optional, but highly recommended).

Main Input

1. Turn back to page 69 (one page flip earlier), then say:

   **"Hmm... 'The boggart's voice sounded a little like a piece of metal dragging across a stone...'
   I find that sound hard to make with my own voice, but I wonder if we could make it using some instruments?"**

2. Invite your learners to suggest ways you could create this sound using the percussion instruments (and/or objects) you have to hand. Take different ideas and experiment until you have a sound similar to this one.
   As you go, remind your learners, or introduce to them, how to correctly use the different instruments available.

Independent/Group Activity

Give each learner or small group a sound effect to create, and invite them to experiment with the different percussion instruments/objects to find a sound that works well.

Provide a reasonable amount of time for them to do so. Circulate and support your learners as needed.

Adaptations

- If you have more time, invite your learners or small groups to create their own sounds for the entire story. You may need to make copies of the short version to share amongst your learners.
- Instead of using instruments, you could take the lesson outdoors and challenge your learners to create sound effects using natural materials.

Plenary

1. Once you are confident every learner/small group has a sound to share for all 8 effects in the story, read the short version found on page 96, prompting the appropriate sound effect every time you read a passage in bold.
   OPTIONAL: Once your learners have practiced it through, you could record it for them to listen back to at a later time.
2. Reward your learners for their work in this lesson by continuing to read the story!

Check In

Talk To Your Partner:

"What have you learnt today?"

Encourage your learners to share their thoughts. **We highly recommend this is the moment you share the Learning Objective with them, if at all.**

The Farmer and the Boggart

Based on a Lincolnshire folk tale
Adapted and written by Chip Colquhoun and Helen Simpson

Farmer Rob **tiptoed down the road** and into a field.

In the field, **the ground in front of him begin to shake... Then it began to swirl... Then it exploded in a burst of mud!**

And there, standing in front of Rob and staring at him with a wide ugly smirk, was a boggart.

The boggart's voice sounded a little like a piece of metal dragging across a stone. "This is my land, farmer! I will let you work on it, but only if you give me everything you grow!

Farmer Rob said he would farm the land if the boggart allowed him to keep half of the food.

The boggart hummed as it thought – a hum that sounded like a wasp trapped in a metal bucket. Then it said "Yes, I will only take half, so you stay and make more."

Rob then asked the boggart whether it wanted the half of the food from above the ground or the half from below the ground.

The boggart hummed again, that gritty waspish sound, then said, "I will take the top half of the plants!"

Farmer Rob **sprinkled the seeds all over the ground**, and worked hard to water the seeds as well. The boggart just stood there and watched.

At last, Farmer Rob sat down beside the field for a rest and wait for the seeds to grow.

The boggart didn't want to wait. It held its hands over the field, and said, "*Acceleration germination!*"

A strange, magical sound filled the air – and, in less than a minute, **all the seeds grew into hundreds of tall, gleaming green plants**.

The boggart leapt forward and **jumped with glee into the tall, gleaming green plants**.

Boggart Sound Effects List

Farmer Rob tiptoeing down the road.

The ground shaking, swirling and exploding.

The boggart sounding like a piece of metal being dragged across a stone.

The boggart humming like a wasp stuck in a metal bucket.

The seeds being sprinkled all over the ground.

A magical sound.

The seeds growing tall.

The boggart jumping into the middle of the plants.

Story First

Ages 4+ PSHE

Someone Like You

Learning Objective(s)

- To identify positive and helpful qualities in oneself and each other.

Resources

Choose one or both of the following...

- A large sheets of plain paper, big enough to trace the outline of any one of your learners.
- Poster-sized sheets of plain paper (e.g. A3).

Starter – *"Do Now!"*

Hooks into learning

1. Invite a learner to lie down on the large sheet of paper so you can trace them.
2. Wonder aloud what Farmer Rob might look like:

"What would Farmer Rob be wearing? What would he be holding?"

3. Invite your learners to contribute to turning the outline into Farmer Rob so that you co-create the image together.

Main Input

1. When you judge that the image of Farmer Rob is finished, draw him a speech bubble and write in it, "It seems the people of Mumby really need someone like me!"
2. Discuss with your learners:

"Why did the people of Mumby need Farmer Rob? What was he like?"

3. As your learners come up with adjectives and other ideas about Farmer Rob and his talents, scribe them around the outline. Alternatively, invite your learners to write ideas on sticky notes, then come up and attach them to it.
4. Then say:

"I think the people of Mumby could have used people like us too. There are a lot of different personalities and talents in this room. What could *you* have helped them with?"

Spend time discussing this altogether or in small groups, helping your learners to identify both what they are like (e.g. kind, helpful, funny) and what they are good at (i.e. their talents).

Independent/Group Activity

Choose one or more of the following...

- Invite your learners to create a "Mumby needs ME!" poster, drawing a portrait of themselves surrounded with statements about their personalities and talents.
- In small groups, invite your learners to draw representations of Mumby village together, then add small characters to represent themselves and their classmates. Suggest that each character has a speech bubble declaring a personality or talent (e.g. "I am Rob and I like to share"). You could also invite them to move around the room to discuss their traits with each other during this activity, and contribute to each other's artworks.

Plenary

- Give your learners time to move around the room and talk about the work that they and the others have done.
- Reflect on all of the different talents and personalities among them.

Check In

Talk To Your Partner:

"What have you learnt today?"

Encourage your learners to share their thoughts. **We highly recommend this is the moment you share the Learning Objective with them, if at all.**

Ages 4+ English
Boggart vs Rumpelstiltskin

Learning Objective(s)

- To listen to and discuss a wide range of stories.
- To become increasingly familiar with key stories, fairy tales, and traditional tales.
- To participate in discussion about books, in both shared and independent reading.
- To explain an understanding of what has been read.

Resources

- Copies of the 'Boggart vs Rumpelstiltskin Sorting Mat' from page 103, enough for one per learner.
- Copies of the 'Boggart vs Rumpelstiltskin Sorting Cards' from page 104, enough for one per learner.
  You can either cut these out for your learners in advance, or supply them with scissors to cut out themselves.
- 3 x exercise hoops OR one extra large copy of the 'Boggart vs Rumpelstiltskin Sorting Mat'.
- Sticky notes and pens/pencils.
- Glue and/or sticky tape.
- A copy of 'Rumpelstiltskin' from page 105, either just for yourself OR per learner.

Prior Knowledge Check

Talk To Your Partner:

"What do you remember happening in the story of 'The Farmer and the Boggart'?"

Encourage your learners to share what they remember.

Main Input

1. Share the story of 'Rumplestiltskin' with your learners, either as shared reading OR by letting them read it independently, depending on the level of your learners.
2. Ask your learners:

"Does the story of 'Rumplestiltskin' remind you of the story of 'The Farmer and the Boggart' in any way?

Encourage them to share their ideas and also expand on them and justify their opinions.

3. Arrange your exercise hoops into a Venn diagram and label one side 'The Farmer and the Boggart' and the other side 'Rumplestiltskin'. OR reveal your large copy of the 'Boggart vs Rumpelstiltskin Sorting Mat'.
4. Ask your learners to recall or point to details about either story, and write each suggestion on a sticky note.
5. Invite your learners to sort the sticky notes into the appropriate spaces of the Venn diagram.

Independent/Group Activity

Share copies of the 'Boggart vs Rumplestiltskin Sorting Mat and Cards' with your learners, either independently or in small groups, and invite them to stick down the Cards in the appropriate spaces.

If you have a more confident class, they could write statements in themselves or add extra statements that are their own ideas.

There's more...

Plenary

- Invite your learners to share their opinions about the two stories, for example...

"What did you like/dislike about the stories?"

"Which story do you prefer, and why?"

"Do you think you think either the boggart or Rumplestiltskin was good in any way?"

Check In

Talk To Your Partner:

"What have you learnt today?"

Encourage your learners to share their thoughts. **We highly recommend this is the moment you share the Learning Objective with them, if at all.**

Boggart vs Rumpelstiltskin

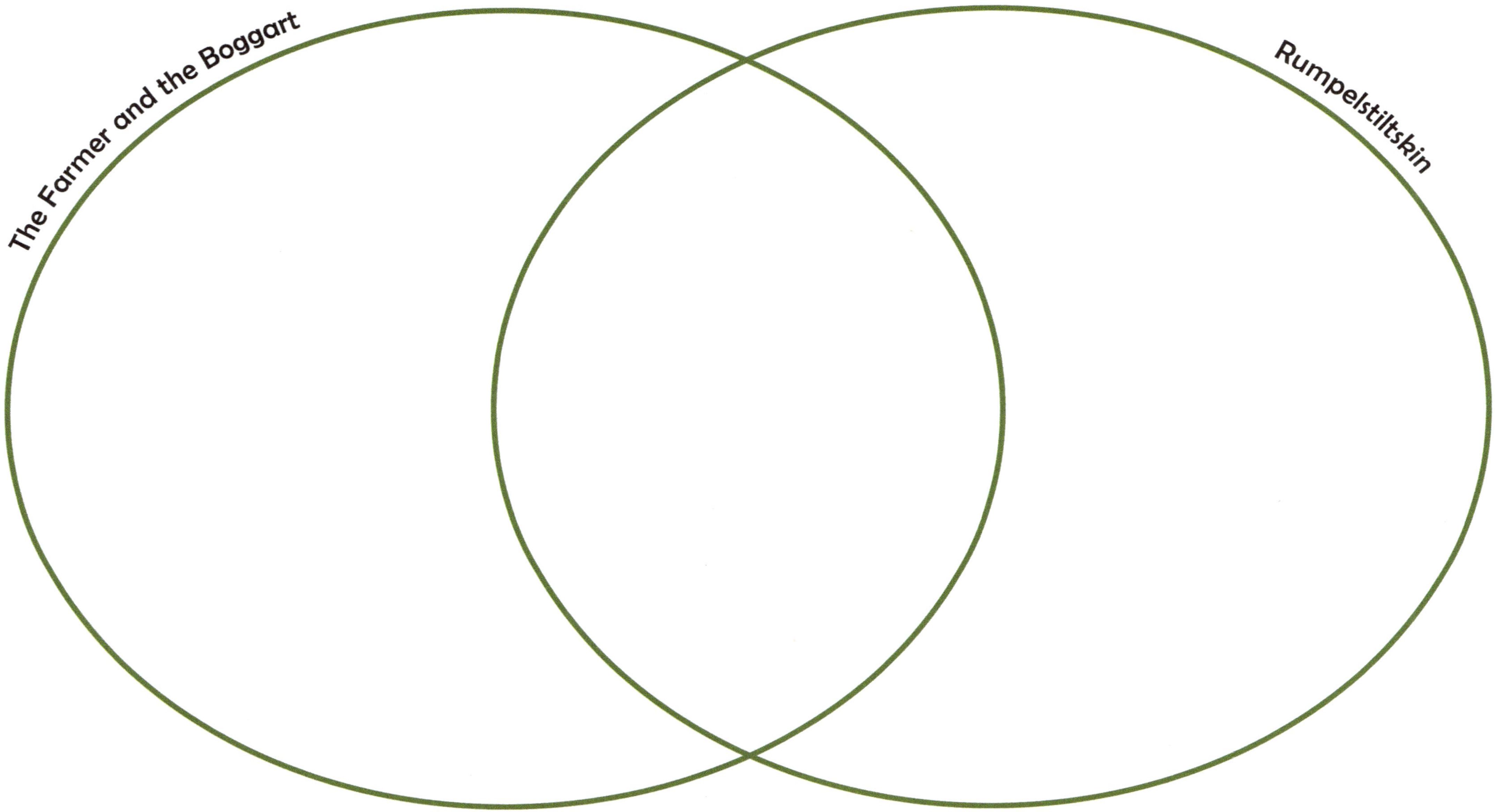

Boggart vs Rumpelstiltskin

There is a strange, unfriendly creature.	There is a clever creature.
A creature helps someone out.	The creature disappears.
The creature gets angry.	Someone gets a 'happily ever after'.
The main character helps others out.	The main character is a farmer.
There is a king.	There is a trick.
A baby is born.	The main character is a girl.

Rumpelstiltskin

Based on a German folk tale
Adapted and written by Chip Colquhoun

A poor miller had a beautiful daughter, and liked to boast that his daughter could spin straw into gold.

One day, the king heard about the miller's daughter. Feeling greedy, the the king locked the girl in a room filled with straw and a spinning wheel, and said, "Turn this straw into gold before morning, or we'll chop off your head!"

The poor girl had no idea how to spin straw into gold. But then, a strange little creature called an 'imp' appeared. The imp looking like a small man with pointy ears, pointy nose, and a pointy chin. He offered to help if the girl could give him something in return.

The girl gave him her necklace, so the imp spun the straw into gold and then left.

When the king returned, he was delighted. But now he wanted more. So the very next day, he locked the girl in a larger room with even more straw.

The imp came back. This time, the girl her ring. So again, the imp spun straw into gold.

On the third night, the king locked the girl in the largest room yet, filled with even more straw. The imp returned, but the girl had nothing left to give. So the imp asked for her first child. Desperate, she agreed.

In the morning, the king was so pleased, he let the girl marry his son, the prince.

Years later, the girl became the queen and had a baby. The imp returned to claim his prize.

The queen begged to keep her child. The imp said, "Yes, but only if you can guess my name after three days!"

The queen sent out messengers, and one overheard the imp singing, "My name is Rumpelstiltskin!"

When the imp returned, the queen guessed correctly. Furious, Rumpelstiltskin stomped his foot so hard that he disappeared forever, leaving the queen and her child in peace.

Story First

Ages 4+ Science

Root Vegetables

Learning Objective(s)

- To identify and name a variety of plants.
- To identify and describe the basic structure of a variety of flowering plants.

Resources

- Root vegetable seeds, e.g. carrot, potato, parsnip, swede, turnip, sweet potato, onion.
- Fully-grown root vegetables to match the seeds.
- Soil, pots, and other planting equipment.

Preparation

Sort the seeds into separate bags by type, but **without labels**.

Starter – *"Do Now!"*

Hooks into learning

1. Show your seeds to your learners, and let them know:

**"Now Farmer Rob has rid the village of the boggart, he's free to start planting seeds to grow into food only for the villagers.
He's got some root vegetable seeds, but he's forgotten which seed is which – so he has no idea what will grow!
How can we find out?"**

2. Draw out the idea that the seeds could be planted to find out what they will grow into.

Prior Knowledge Check

1. Ask your learners:

"Does anyone remember the boggart's spell to grow vegetables quickly?"

2. Once you have the answer, try waving your hands over the seeds and saying "Acceleration germination!" a few times, perhaps inviting your learners to help for the second time or more.

Main Input

1. Wonder aloud why the seeds aren't changing. As your learners identify that the magic isn't working, discuss with them what could be done instead to get these seeds growing into plants.
2. Draw out that they need soil, water, air, sunlight... and time! Let them know:

"The boggart didn't have much time or patience, but we need to have time and patience to grow vegetables."

3. Plant the seeds together in groups, the same seed type in each pots or group of pots, without telling your learners which plants they are.
4. Discuss with your learners what they expect will happen to the seeds over the next a few weeks.
5. On a display board or large piece of paper, draw a diagram introducing your learners to the parts of a plant: roots, stem, leaves, and flower.
6. Finish focusing on the root. Explain that root vegetables are so called because we eat the root, and reveal your fully-grown root vegetables.
7. Take some time naming the vegetables with your learners, cutting them open to see inside, and discussing whether your learners have tried them.

Independent/Group Activity

1. Over the following weeks, occasionally check in with your learners to observe how the root vegetables grow. You can build a rota for individual learners/pairs/groups to record these observations, or do them as a unified group.
2. During the observing weeks, occasionally remind your learners that you can't tell which vegetable is which because the vegetables are the root and so below ground. However, you may wish to play a guessing game with them.
3. When it is time to harvest the vegetables, allow your learners to observe that the roots are the edible part, and identify which vegetables are which. Did anyone guess correctly?

Check In

Talk To Your Partner:

"What have you learnt today?"

Encourage your learners to share their thoughts. **We highly recommend this is the moment you share the Learning Objective with them, if at all.**

Ages 4+ DT
Farmer Rob's New Farm

Learning Objective(s)

- To understand where food comes from.

Resources

- A range of fruit and vegetables, ideally grown in your country and/or local area.
- A range of manufactured foods (e.g. pasta, bread, flour, biscuits... anything that's not grown).
- Copies of 'Farmer Rob's New Farm' from page 110, ideally on A3, enough for one per learner and yourself.

Prior Knowledge Check

Talk To Your Partner:

"What did Farmer Rob grow on his farm during the story? Are there any other plants he could grow on his farm for food?"

Encourage your learners to share their thoughts.

Starter – *"Do Now!"*

Hooks into learning

1. Lay out a copy of 'Farmer Rob's New Farm', then say:

"Now that Farmer Rob has made a new home in Mumby and has a new farm, he needs our help to plan what to grow and where to put it. So I wonder... Which foods grow on farms?"

2. Show them the range of foods from the resources to begin a discussion about which foods are grown and which are manufactured.
3. Let your learners know that all foods come from somewhere, they don't just appear in shops – but some foods are grown while others are made up of different ingredients.

Main Input

1. Once you have established together which foods are grown and which are not, use a display board or large piece of paper to draw an outline of a tree, an outline of a bush, and an outline of patch of soil.
2. Inviting help from your learners, sort the fruits and vegetables onto those grown on a tree, a bush, or in soil, drawing them in their correct source.
   If a learner makes another suggestion for a source that you have not brought with you, you can still add it to your picture.
3. Keep this completed sorting activity available for your learners to refer to during the Independent/Group Activity.
4. OPTIONAL: Discuss with your learners whether Farmer Rob should have some livestock on his farm, and what they could produce for him (e.g. a herd of cows to produce milk, butter, and cheese).

Independent/Group Activity

Encourage your learners to create a plan using copies of 'Farmer Rob's New Farm' to show what they would grow and how it would grow – e.g. apples on trees, carrots in soil, etc. Use the A3 planning frame available, or create one of your own. They label the farm plan when they have drawn the images

Plenary

- Lay out your learners' work around the room, then let them go around looking at ech other's work. If they have a positive comment to make about it, you may wish to allow them to write it on a sticky note to leave with the work.

Check In

Talk To Your Partner:

"What have you learnt today?"

Encourage your learners to share their thoughts. **We highly recommend this is the moment you share the Learning Objective with them, if at all.**

Farmer Rob’s New Farm

Make a plan for Farmer Rob. What will he grow? Where will he grow it? Fill each field with a crop.

Design Farmer Rob a farmhouse here!

The Chocolate Journey

Place of origin: The Ivory Coast, Africa

Destination: Mumby, Lincolnshire, UK

1. Pods grown on trees

2. Beans taken from pods

3. Beans shipped to UK

4. Beans roasted & mixed in a factory

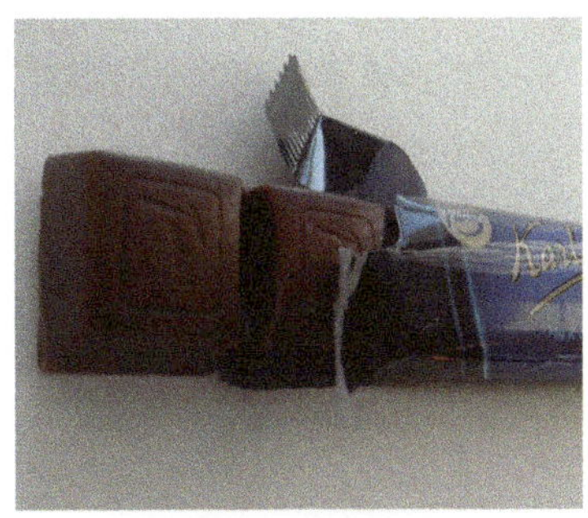

5. Packaged in a factory

6. Truck to Mumby

7. Product in Mumby village shop

Story Pause

Ages 7+ Maths
The Commutative Law

Learning Objective(s)

- To understand and use the commutative law.
- To understand when the commutative law cannot be used.

Resources

- Small counters, or something that can be used as counters (e.g. balls of modeling clay, pieces of paper, etc), enough for at least 15 per learner or small group.
- Small pots for the counters to go in, enough for at least 3 per learner or small group.
- Paper and pens.
- A display board.
- A large calculator OR onscreen calculator (optional).

Preparation

For each learner or small group, fill their pots with an equal number of counters – but make sure each learner/group's pots contain a different combination of quantities.

You needn't give out all the counters/pots at once.

For example, if you have six small groups, you might prepare...

- one lot of 3 pots containing 6 counters each
- one lot of 4 pots containing 3 counters each
- one lot of 4 pots containing 5 counters each
- one lot of 4 pots containing 6 counters each
- one lot of 5 pots containing 3 counters each
- one lot of 5 pots containing 4 counters each

Starter – *"Do Now!"*

Hooks into learning

1. Read/continue/re-read 'The Farmer and the Boggart' to the mark **<7+ M1>** (optional, but highly recommended).
2. Reveal one set of pots, declaring each pot to be a wheelbarrow and each counter a peapod. Count the 'peapods' in just two or three 'wheelbarrows'.
3. Talk to Your Partner:

   "If all the wheelbarrows hold the same number of pods, can you work out how many pods we have in total without counting them all?"

   Encourage them to write down their solutions.

Main Input

1. Ask your learners to volunteer an explanation for how they arrived at their answer. Draw out their multiplication (e.g. 3 times 6), but write it up the reverse way on your display board (i.e. 6 times 3).
2. Ask your learners,

   "Oh, I'm sorry, I think I wrote that down wrong. Is that what they just said to me?"

   If your learners don't pick up the difference straight away, ask the volunteer to repeat what they said.
3. Ask your learners if they think you'll get a different answer, then ask,

   "Shall we find out?"

   Work out the answers to both forms of the equation, ideally using a calculator so your learners are immediately confident that the answer is correct.
4. Explain that this is 'The Commutative Law': we can swap the numbers around when multiplying, and still get the same answer.

Independent/Group Activity

Challenge your learners to collect the 'wheelbarrow x peapod' equations by asking each other, but only writing down 'peapod x wheelbarrow' equations. OPTIONAL: encourage them to solve the equations on paper too.

We recommend you do this with your learners staying in one place, to create a 'market day' vibe!

There's more...

Plenary

1. Point to individual learners/groups, but ask other individual/group to volunteer the equation for how many peapods they have. Then check it against the answer from those you've indicated, celebrating all successful uses of the commutative law.
2. Ask your learners,

"Shall we try getting an equal number of peapods in every wheelbarrow that we've got? What will we need to know first?"

3. Draw out the need to add up all the wheelbarrows and all the peapods. If any/all have written down the equations for every set of wheelbarrows, they should have all these numbers ready to total.
4. Ask your learners,

"What type of operation do we need to work this out? Addition, subtraction, multiplication, or division?"

5. After drawing out division, ask for the number of wheelbarrows, and write this on your display board followed by the divide symbol. Then ask for the number of peapods.
6. Ask your learners,

"Will this work?"

7. Discuss their thoughts, concluding with the fact that the commutative law doesn't work for all operations.
8. OPTIONAL: Invite your learners to work out whether the law works with addition and/or subtraction.
9. Reward your learners for their work in this lesson by continuing to read the story!

Check In

Talk To Your Partner:

"What have you learnt today?"

Encourage your learners to share their thoughts. **We highly recommend this is the moment you share the Learning Objective with them, if at all.**

Story First

Ages 7+ Science
Reversible & Irreversible Changes

Learning Objective(s)

- To investigate and understand reversible and irreversible changes.

Resources

- A range of materials with responses under heat and subsequent cooling that will be easy and safe for your learners to test (but ***not*** paper), such as...

  chocolate - jelly - cotton wool - bread

- Safe heat sources that your learners can use, including protective equipment where necessary.
- Paper and writing tools.
- **Optional, but highly recommended**: cut/mold your materials into boggart shapes.

Preparation

Optional: as part of a DT precursor, allow your learners to create some chocolate/jelly molds in the shape of boggarts.

Prior Knowledge Check

Choose one or both of the following...

- Encourage your learners to show the molecules in a solid, liquid, and/or gas, either as individuals or in small groups, either through drawing, written descriptions, body movement, or their choice for each.
- Encourage your learners to share what they remember about the end of 'The Farmer and the Boggart' story.

Starter – *"Do Now!"*

Hooks into learning

Ask your learners:

"Can you put the events of 'The Farmer and the Boggart' in reverse order?"

Use this activity to prompt a discussion as to the meaning of 'reverse'.

Main Input

1. Inform your learners:

"To celebrate Farmer Rob's triumph over the boggart, the villagers of Mumby have decided to create a special festival to tell the story! They want a material to show the boggart that's more interesting than paper, but which will disappear in the same way the boggart did. I thought I might try chocolate..."

   Discuss whether this is a good choice.

2. Experiment by melting some chocolate, then ask your learners what they think will happen when the chocolate cools.

"So has the boggart disappeared as in the story?"

3. Draw out the conclusion that melting the chocolate is a 'reversible change'. What the villagers of Mumby need is the opposite: an '***irreversible*** change'.

Independent/Group Activity

Split your learners into invididuals/small groups, then distribute the materials, paper, and writing tools among them. Challenge them to...

1. write a prediction for each material as to whether it will demonstrate a reversible change or an irreversible change; then
2. test their predictions.

Plenary

- Encourage your learners to share their findings using the language of reversible and irreversible changes.

Check In

Talk To Your Partner:

"What have you learnt today?"

Encourage your learners to share their thoughts. **We highly recommend this is the moment you share the Learning Objective with them, if at all.**

Ages 7+ PSHE
Resilience

Learning Objective(s)

- To understand what it means to be resilient.

Resources

Choose one or both of the following...

- A large sheets of plain paper, big enough to trace the outline of any one of your learners.
- Poster-sized sheets of plain paper (e.g. A3).
- **Optional** (for the Prior Knowledge Check): dictionaries and/or internet-connected devices.

Prior Knowledge Check

Talk To Your Partner:

"What does resilient mean? If you're not sure, see if you can find out!"

Allow your learners to use the dictionaries and/or online search tools, directing them towards those tools if required.

Starter – *"Do Now!"*

Hooks into learning

Talk To Your Partner:

"Can you think of a character from 'The Farmer and the Boggart' story who was resilient? Why do you think that?"

Main Input

1. Either draw an outline of a person on a sheet of A3 or your display board, or trace one of your learners onto the large sheet of paper.
2. Discuss with your learners:

   "What does being resilient look like from the outside?"

   As your learners come up with adjectives and other ideas, scribe them around the outline. Take just two or three.

   Invite them to remember their idea of a resilient character from the story during this activity.
3. Then say:

   "What does being resilient feel like on the *in*side?"

   Again, scribe just two or three of these ideas on the inside of the outline.

   And again, encourage them to think from the perspective of their chosen resilient character from the story.

Independent/Group Activity

Invite your learners to create a similar poster showing how resilience feels on the inside compared with how it looks on the outside. They can either use A3 or work in small groups to trace themselves onto larger sheets of paper.

You may wish to challenge them to come up with a certain number.

Plenary

- Give your learners time to move around the room and talk about the work that they and the others have done.
- Reflect on how you will recognise resilience in each other and around your setting.

Check In

Talk To Your Partner:

"What have you learnt today?"

Encourage your learners to share their thoughts. **We highly recommend this is the moment you share the Learning Objective with them, if at all.**

Story First

Ages 7+ English:
Simile Seeker

Learning Objective(s)

- To use appropriate and effective similes.

Resources

- Copies of the illustration from page 68, enough for one per learner or small group.
- Writing materials.

Prior Knowledge Check

Talk To Your Partner:

"What details do you remember of the boggart from the story of 'The Farmer and the Boggart'?"

Starter – *"Do Now!"*

Hooks into learning

1. Distribute the copies of the illustration, then ask your learners to discuss in small groups:

"Using the word 'like' or 'as', what can you compare the boggart to?"

Optional: Provide a couple of examples, such as...

"As big as a cow."

"Voice like a wasp in a metal bucket."

2. Take some time for them to feedback and discuss their thoughts with the wider group:

"Do we like that comparison? Does it work?"

Main Input

1. Explain that comparisons using the word 'like' or 'as' are known as similes.
2. Discuss with your learners:

"The story doesn't give us much description of Farmer Rob... What similes could we use for him?"

As you gather answers, remind them that they can consider his physicality using the illustration as a guide, but also his personality.

Independent Activity

Encourage your learners to write similes for...

1. The boggart
2. Farmer Rob
3. The barman
4. Rob's grandma

Plenary

Ask your learners:

"Can we also use simile for settings? Have a go at writing 2 simile sentences for the village."

Check In

Talk To Your Partner:

"What have you learnt today?"

Encourage your learners to share their thoughts. **We highly recommend this is the moment you share the Learning Objective with them, if at all.**

Story First

Ages 7+ Geography
Where does our food come from?

Learning Objective(s)

- To understand trade routes in urban and rural settings.

Resources

- Copies of 'The Chocolate Journey' from page 111 to distribute among your learners in small groups.
- Paper and writing/drawing tools.
- Reference books and/or online access for researching food origins and journeys.

Prior Knowledge Check

Talk To Your Partner:

"Who can remember what foods were grown by Farmer Rob in the story of 'The Farmer and the Boggart'?"

Encourage your learners to share what they remember.

Starter – *"Do Now!"*

Hooks into learning

Talk To Your Partner:

"What other foods do you think the villagers of Mumby might want?"

Main Input

1. Spend some time discussing your learners' lists from the Starter, taking time to break down any composite foods into separate components (e.g. 'pizza' into 'bread', 'cheese', 'tomato', etc.

   If it isn't contributed by your learners, be sure to mention chocolate yourself.

2. Ask your learners:

   "Are there any foods on our list that could *not* be grown by Farmer Rob? Where could they come from?"

3. When chocolate is discussed, point out:

   "I happen to know the journey chocolate takes to get to a village like Mumby..."

4. Share and discuss 'The Chocolate Journey'.
5. Model the research and creation of a food journey for another food item on your list, involving your learners in the process.

Independent/Group Activity

Set each individual or small group a number of food items from the list to investigate, and challenge them to research their origins and journeys, then create their own journey sheets.

Plenary

- Bring your learners back together to discuss each other's work.
- Altogether, consider and discuss any adjustments that may need to be made to deliver the foods to big cities like London.

Check In

Talk To Your Partner:

"What have you learnt today?"

Encourage your learners to share their thoughts. **We highly recommend this is the moment you share the Learning Objective with them, if at all.**

Story First

Ages 7+ DT

Food Packaging

Learning Objective(s)

- To design appealing packaging.

Resources

- Several examples of food packaging (boxes, packets, etc).
- Plain paper.
- Card.
- Writing/drawing tools.

Prior Knowledge Check

This may not be required if you have already tried the Geography lesson on pages 122–123

Talk To Your Partner:

"Who can remember what foods were grown by Farmer Rob in the story of 'The Farmer and the Boggart'?"

Encourage your learners to share what they remember.

Starter – *"Do Now!"*

Hooks into learning

Ask your learners:

"What recipes could you create with the foods grown by Farmer Rob?"

Discuss ideas altogether, considering the utensils and any other ingredients needed to make them.

Main Input

1. Challenge your learners to design some packaging to go with a dish you've all discussed that they like the sound of the best.
2. Discuss with your learners:

"What needs to be on the packaging when we are designing packaging for food?"

Create a list of things that the packaging will need, such as...

- Name of product
- Name of company
- Picture of product when made
- Ingredients
- Recipe
- Nutritional info

3. Model the creation of a plan on paper, then set them the Independent/Group Activity. *You may wish to model the creation of sample packaging too using your card.*

Independent/Group Activity

Allow your learners to design their packaging on paper first, either individually or in small groups. Those who complete this first task may then create a model of their design using card.

Plenary

Bring your learners back together to discuss each other's work.

Check In

Talk To Your Partner:

"What have you learnt today?"

Encourage your learners to share their thoughts. **We highly recommend this is the moment you share the Learning Objective with them, if at all.**

About Your Storytellers

Chip Colquhoun began storytelling professionally in 2007. He's since performed in 10 countries, presented Traditional Tales for the Oxford Reading Tree online, performed regularly at Glastonbury Festival, and represented the Roald Dahl Story Museum on ITV. He also wrote the EU's guidance on using storytelling in schools. He lives in the former residence of Samuel Pepys, England's most famous diarist, up in Cambridgeshire with his wife Emma and kittens Tito and Pippa. For his free creative writing and newsletter of tips for educators to inspire reluctant/resistant readers, visit storytellerchip.com

Korky Paul began his career scribbling for an advertising agency in Cape Town. His first illustration job was a book teaching English, then a pop-up called *The Crocodile and the Dumper Truck* – but it was his work on *Winnie the Witch* that won the Children's Book Award in 1987 and made him a much-loved figure in the world of children's books. He's since illustrated for Oxford University Press, Penguin, Random House, and others. He lives in Oxford with his wife Susan. To keep up with his work, visit korkypaul.com

Mario Coelho was born on the Brazilian island of Florianopolis. He worked as an artist and designer in the textile industry before moving to England in 1985. After completing a course in children's book illustration run by Korky Paul, Mario began receiving several commissions, starting with an edition of Oscar Wilde's *The Canterville Ghost* published by Oxford University Press. For more examples of his work, or to commission him yourself, visit mariocoelho.co.uk

Helen Simpson has been a teacher for 13 years, working mainly across the EYFS and KS1 age ranges. She enjoys teaching through drama and storytelling, which led her to meet Chip and start working with him to help teachers to use more stories in their classrooms. Her favourite things in school are stories, maps, Mantle of the Expert, teaching outdoors, and of course literacy. She has been the English lead at her last two schools and has an interest in early reading and writing, helping children to love books from the very start.

Rob Small has worked in schools in Milton Keynes and North Buckinghamshire for 11 years. He has taught across Key Stages 1 and 2, as well as spending some time in EYFS. Currently he works in a small village school as a class teacher and Literacy lead. Promoting a love of literacy and reading is one of his key aims – and, with enthusiastic lessons and an exciting range of texts, he makes this happen. Rob has worked with other teachers, authors, and booksellers to help children to grow their love of reading.

Additional Image Attributions

The following images used in this publication were made available under Creative Commons 'ShareAlike' and 'Attribution' licences, and were cropped where necessary:

Mahula tree (Madhuca longifolia) of Odisha **by Aditya Mahar**
Coconut tree photo **by Kiruthika Off**
Vine Jungle El Yunque National Forest **by EgorovaSvetlana**
Chisapani Devisthan Temple Kuchkuche Jungle Sauraha Chitwan Nepal Rajesh Dhungana (4) **by Rajesh Dhungana**
Giant Red Bug (Macrocheraia grandis) male nymph **by Bernard DUPONT**
Red panda feeding on bamboo, Bratislava, Jan 2023 **by Soggy Pandas**
Coucang **by Aprisonsan**
Indian Leopard **by Sipuwildlife**
Oak Tree, Oakwood Park, London, N14 **by Christine Matthews**
Weeping willow, Dyffryn gardens **by M J Roscoe**
European beech (Fagus sylvatica) in Humlamaden 1516 **by Gunnar Creutz**
Woodland Path to Burial Ground **by Billy McCrorie**
Stag Beetle **by Andy Reago & Chrissy McClarren**
Rabbit (Oryctolagus cuniculus) Skomer **by Charles J. Sharp**
Eichhörnchen (Sciurus vulgaris) Konstantinhügel Wiener Prater **by Manfred Werner**
Fox at the British Wildlife Centre, Newchapel, Surrey **by Peter Trimming**
Hare in Solna, Sweden 2014 **by Jopparn**
Jungle cat **by Davidvraju**
Gaur Bos gaurus **by Raju Kasambe**
Village Shop **by Alan Hughes**
Village Church **by Robert Graham**
Woodcote Village Green War Memorial **by Marathon**
Butley, houses and village sign **by Bikeboy**
Village school, Hovingham **by Gordon Hatton**
B1083 Woodbridge Road & Sutton Village Sign **by Geographer**
Village Farm **by Michael Dibb**
Chiddingstone Village Pub - The Castle Inn **by Michael Gaylard**
Sao Tome Ponta Figo Hike Cocoa Pods 5 **by Chuck Moravec**
Cocao beans and pod **by gailhampshire**
Cadbury Chudovo **by Дар Ветер**
Fazer Blue chocolate bar **by TTKK**
Belgian chocolate shop in Brussels **by Zorro2212**
Cargo ship 1 **by Sciencia58**

The following images used in this publication were made available under Creative Commons 'ShareAlike' and 'Attribution' licences, and were enhanced for brightness:

All Gond Art **by Sumita Roy Dutta**

Ma*hoo*sive thanks to the many creators using Creative Commons, who make endeavours like this both possible and affordable for our education community. 😀

Visit commons.wikimedia.org **for more details and images.**

Milton Keynes UK
Ingram Content Group UK Ltd.
UKHW052244140824
446854UK00006B/51

9 781915 703293